TWAYNE'S WORLD AUTHORS SERIES

A Survey of the World's Literature

Sylvia E. Bowman, Indiana University

GENERAL EDITOR

JAPAN

Roy E. Teele, The University of Texas at Austin

EDITOR

Dazai Osamu

TWAS 348

Photo by Tamura Shigeru

Dazai Osamu

Dazai Osamu

By JAMES A. O'BRIEN

The University of Wisconsin

TWAYNE PUBLISHERS
A DIVISION OF G. K. HALL & CO., BOSTON

Library of Congress Cataloging in Publication Data

O'Brien, James Aloysius, 1936 -
  Dazai Osamu.

  (Twayne's world authors series ; TWAS 348 : Japan)
  Bibliography: p. 173 - 75.
  Includes index.
  1. Dazai, Osamu, pseud. — Criticism and interpreta-
tion.
PL825.A8Z77   895.6'3'4   74-20998
ISBN 0-8057-2664-0

895.63
D2770

Contents

About the Author

James A. O'Brien came to the study of Japanese literature after receiving the B.A. and M.A. in English literature. During the course of his graduate career in Japanese, he studied at Indiana University, The University of Michigan, Columbia University, and The Tokyo University of Education. He received the Ph. D. from Indiana University in 1969 for his dissertation on Dazai Osamu, a study which formed the basis of the present book.

In addition to this major study he has written articles on Dazai in both English and Japanese. He also specializes in the study and translation of modern Japanese poetry; during the past academic year he has been at work on the poetry of Murano Shiro under a grant from the Social Science Research Council. He is serving as editor-in-chief of the *Dictionary of Japanese Literature*, part of a series of volumes on various national literatures commissioned by the Greenwood Press.

Dr. O'Brien has served on the faculty of The Department of East Asian Languages and Literature at The University of Wisconsin since 1968. He currently holds the rank of associate professor in the department.

Preface

Dazai Osamu was born Tsushima Shuji on June 19, 1909, in Aomori, the northernmost prefecture of the main Japanese island of Honshu. His birthplace was the small town of Kanagi, located at the base of the Tsugaru Peninsula midway between Aomori Bay and the Sea of Japan.

On June 19, 1948, precisely thirty-nine years later, the Tokyo police pulled the corpse of Dazai Osamu from the Tamagawa Canal. Along with Dazai they found the body of Yamazaki Tomie, the author's mistress. Yamazaki possibly lured an unwilling Dazai into the swift stream; more likely, Dazai deliberately joined his mistress in the traditional act of *joshi*, or double suicide.

During the thirty-nine years of his life Dazai constantly threw himself into acts of desperation. He appears to have attempted suicide at least four times before his final act. He drank heavily and, for a time, suffered an addiction to drugs. Associated with illegal radical movements, he was picked up several times by the police for questioning. Married and divorced once, he married again and fathered a family, only to find himself dissatisfied with domesticity. He escaped from his family by carrying on several affairs, the last with Yamazaki Tomie.

Dazai's life has fascinated the Japanese public. Books with such titles as *Dazai Osamu: Human Being, The Story of Dazai Osamu,* and *The Sayings of Dazai Osamu* have flowed from the pens of Dazai's literary friends. Dazai's second wife, Michiko, has written several interesting reminiscences about her wayward husband, and the author's illegitimate daughter appeared on Japanese television in 1969, giving her reactions upon the occasion of a visit to her father's birthplace. A rumor several years ago had the local librarian in Kanagi contemplating a book on Dazai. The materials for a biographical study, then, are abundantly available, and Dazai is the type of writer who invites a biographical treatment.

A study of the philosophical and literary sources of Dazai's art is also a feasible undertaking. Dazai was delightfully eclectic in his reading and his literary enthusiasms. During his youth, he learned of democracy and communism as Japan, in the 1920's, underwent a period of liberalism. In the late 1930's and throughout the war years he read the Bible with intense interest. At different stages in his life he picked up a knowledge of certain segments of Japanese literature — of Saikaku and Basho, of *rakugo* storytelling, and of fairy tales and folk legends. Fascinated with Western literature, Dazai found suggestions of plots for his own work in Shakespeare and Schiller.

A number of Japanese scholars — Okuno Tateo, Sako Junichiro and Saegusa Yasutaka come to mind most readily — have examined the way in which these and other diverse influences affected Dazai's course as a writer. The approach of these critics tends to be topical and thematic. They show, for example, how Dazai responded to Marxism and Christianity; they discuss such matters as the author's sense of guilt, his decadence, and his ideal of service toward his readers.

Few, if any, Japanese critics have practiced the more formal kinds of literary criticism on Dazai. Indeed, Dazai resists serious, sustained attempts at this type of criticism. He will, for example, shift the narrative point of view in a single work for reasons that would appall a Henry James or a Percy Lubbock. Sometimes he shifts the narrative point of view, not in response to artistic or technical requirements, but simply to avoid boring himself.

In discussing the writings of Dazai Osamu, one must make constant reference to the life upon which the writings are more or less directly based. Dazai's skill as a creative writer manifests itself principally in his style; his talents for organizing plot or creating a fictional world are relatively meager. To study Dazai means to study the way in which he uses language to tell and retell the story of his own life.

But Dazai is not merely a skillful autobiographer. He takes himself as his principal subject, yet composes a series of works far more diverse and varied than a conventional autobiography. He sees himself in many ways and in many guises. That he can even see himself in a monkey or a badger will suggest the distance between his kind of writing and autobiography.

This book approaches Dazai principally through examining the series of self-images that emerge in his writings. Dazai's life readily divides into five periods, each of which forms the subject of a chapter in this book. Each of these chapters is in turn divided into two parts: a brief biographical sketch and critical discussion (with plot summaries) of the main works composed in the particular period. The conventional analytic tools of academic criticism are employed on occasion, but the principal effort is given over to detecting the will-o'-the-wisp image of Dazai himself.

Finally, a word about the limitations of this book. Most readers will find it necessary to approach Dazai in translation. A few translations are available and most are well done. The reader intrigued by Dazai should consult these translations, using as a guide the bibliography at the end of this book. At the same time I must caution that such a reader will possibly find himself unpersuaded of my view of Dazai. That view is rooted in my response to Dazai's writing style, in particular the intimate tone and deft comic swerves of that style. I doubt that even the most skillful translator can convey these effects precisely in English. To an unfortunate extent the reader who lacks a command of Japanese must accept my word as to the nature of Dazai's art.

A final limitation concerns the works of Dazai necessarily omitted in this study. Dazai's works, short stories and sketches for the most part, fill twelve substantial volumes, and my treatment of this corpus is essentially limited to those better-known works for which I have developed an appreciation. At times, especially in the early chapters, I have included an obscure work that appealed to me or pertained closely to my argument. I must add that I have omitted one major work that conceivably should be included. This is *Sanetomo, Minister of the Right,* a novel composed during World War II. One reading of the novel, with its ponderous "medieval" style, has convinced me to withhold comment for the time being. I felt it unwise to include in a critical book on Dazai a lengthy work for which I have not developed any appreciable critical understanding.

Acknowledgments

This study has benefited immensely from the labors of the leading scholar of Dazai, Okuno Tateo. Okuno's careful annotations to *The Complete Works* have provided me with information that I could hardly have gathered on my own; in addition, his critical writings on Dazai have been an invaluable stimulus. I have also been helped by the studies of Bessho, Dan, Fukuda, Itagaki, Kamei, Saegusa, and Sugimori. Professor Donald Keene's article on Dazai has been useful, and his translations of *No Longer Human* and *The Setting Sun* first introduced me (just a decade ago) to Dazai.

Much of the research for this book was carried out in preparation for writing my doctoral dissertation for the department of East Asian languages and literatures at Indiana University. I wish to thank the members of my doctoral committee, Professors Wu-chi Liu, Toyoaki Uehara, Kenneth Yasuda, and N. Nabeshima for their guidance and encouragement. I owe a special debt to Professor Roy E. Teele, the Japanese Editor of Twayne's World Authors Series, for cogent advice on revising my manuscript and for a painstaking job of editing. Professor Teele was instrumental in helping me develop a perspective on a writer I once believed could not be put in perspective.

Financial assistance also played its part in helping me complete the study. My doctoral research in Japan was supported by a Fulbright-Hays Award in 1966 - 1967 and a National Defense Education Fellowship in 1967 - 1968. The East Asian Studies Committee of the University of Wisconsin provided me with travel funds for a trip to Japan for additional research in the summer of 1971.

Finally, I wish to thank the editors of *Critique* for permission to use my article "Dazai Osamu: Comic Writer," which appeared in vol. XII, no. 1, of that journal.

JAMES A. O'BRIEN

The University of Wisconsin

Chronology

1909   Tsushima Shuji born on June 19 in Kanagi, a town in Aomori, the northernmost prefecture of the main Japanese island of Honshu.

1916   Enters the Kanagi Grade School.

1923   Death of his father, Genemon. Dazai enters the Prefectural Middle School at Aomori City.

1925   Usually considered the year during which Dazai, now seventeen by the Japanese reckoning of age, began thinking seriously of becoming a writer.

1927   Enters the literature department of the Hirosaki Higher School.

1930   Matriculates at Tokyo University to study French literature. Attempts to commit double suicide with hostess from a Ginza café in the sea at Enoshima.

1931   Allowed by family to marry Koyama Hatsuyo, a geisha friend from his higher school days.

1935   Attempts suicide at Kamakura. Suffers appendicitis attack.

1936 - Period of recovery from appendicitis operation at Funabashi,
1937   Chiba Prefecture. Publication of first important collection, *Final Years*. Suffers from drug addiction. Confined to hospitals and a mental institution during part of this time.

1937   Unsuccessful suicide attempt with Hatsuyo at Minakami Hot Spring. After returning to Tokyo, Dazai and Hatsuyo separate. Publishes "Human Lost" and *The Flower of Buffoonery*.

1937 - Quiescent period in Dazai's writing career.
1938

1939   Marriage to Ishihara Michiko of Kofu. Moves with his bride back to Tokyo and settles in Mitaka Village.

1939   Period of considerable activity for Dazai.

1940   Publishes "Das Gemeine," "One Hundred Views of Mount Fuji," and "Run Melos."

1941 *"Eight Views of Tokyo," "Beggar-Student," "The Indict-ment."*

1944 *Tsugaru.*

1945 *A Retelling of the Tales from the Provinces, A Collection of Fairy Tales.* Evacuates Tokyo along with family, first for Kofu, then for Kanagi.

1946 Returns to Mitaka home.

1947 Affairs with Ota Shizuko and Yamazaki Tomie. "Villon's Wife" and *The Setting Sun* published.

1948 Double suicide with Yamazaki Tomie. "Good-bye" and *No Longer Human* published.

CHAPTER 1

Before Final Years *(1909-1930)*

I *Modern Historical Trends*

IN 1868, after two and one-half centuries of international isolation and domestic feudalism, Japan turned away from its past and struck out in an entirely new direction. Almost overnight the government of the Meiji Reformation opened the way to foreign intercourse of various kinds and began forging within the country a modern unified state. In the century since the Reformation, Japan has undergone a series of relatively violent shifts and turns, a reflection in part of the abruptness with which it first appeared upon the stage of modern history.

In general terms, a historian might speak of modern Japan as a battleground between the conflicting ideologies of liberalism and authoritarianism. Roughly the first two decades of the Meiji Period, beginning in 1868, were a time of awakening and possibility, a sharp contrast to the rigidity of the social order during the previous centuries of Tokugawa rule. In Meiji, men from the lower echelons of the samurai class found themselves in official positions of power and responsibility; students with the aptitude and energy, regardless of their class origins, were eligible to attend the best schools and universities and graduate to attractive careers; intellectuals anxious to extend their vision beyond the shoreline of the Japanese islands could be sent abroad to study under government sponsorship.

In 1890, the issuance of the Imperial Rescript on Education symbolized a transition already well under way from fascination with foreign nations and cultures to a concern for harnessing Japanese energies even more than before to the task of building a strong nation-state. Within a few years, Japan proved it had mastered the technique of Western nationalism by prosecuting two major wars to a successful end. The nation continued to thrive through World War I; having joined the Allied Powers, Japan emerged from Versailles a major world power.

During the 1920's the country joined much of the rest of the world in moving away from militant nationalism and imperialism. A policy of international peace and constitutional government gained favor, and calls for the establishment of socialism — whether Marxist or Christian — were commonly voiced in Japanese public life. But the rise of an occasionally fanatic militarism early in the 1930's abruptly cut down the socialism and radicalism that had struggled to assert itself in the 1920's.

One manifestation of the radicalism of the 1920's was the rise of the tenant-farmer union. During the Tokugawa Period, the farmer occupied a relatively high official position in the Neo-Confucian social order; but in reality he simply bore the brunt of supporting an economy based on agriculture. A shift in the farmer's relation to the government occurred with the advent of the Meiji government, but the general beneficiary of this shift from the very beginning to World War II was the landlord rather than the farmer. Of course, a great number of farmers owned all the land they worked or worked their own and someone else's land. But a considerable group — perhaps 20 to 30 percent of the farmers — worked the land solely as tenants. This group was subject to the usual hazards of tenantry, and government policy often seemed deliberately contrived to favor the landlord over his tenant. The landlords, taking advantage of their close ties with government, lobbied with notable success for substantial decreases in taxation rates on their lands from the beginning of Meiji into the 1920's. The tenants, their interests represented by no one, continued throughout this time to pay the landlord 50 percent of the crop in taxes.

At first the Christian Socialists — effective organizers of urban workers — set about the task of organizing these farmers. By the 1920's the Marxists had taken over this task, and by 1922 had managed to forge a national union. Before the end of the decade almost 400,000 tenants had enrolled from a population of four million families. By the time the government finally cracked down early in the 1930's, there had occurred a number of riots so violent that landlords were often compelled to call for police protection.

II *Proletarian Literature*

Dazai Osamu does not fit easily into the history of modern Japanese literature. Certain literary currents, the I-novel, for example, must be brought into any discussion of Dazai's place in modern Japanese fiction;[1] but almost any subject other than Dazai — be it a school, a doctrine, a style, or whatever — can only be used as a contrast, that is to say, as a definition of what Dazai is not. As I hope to show, Dazai, as a Japanese literary phenomenon, is truly sui generis. Possibly no writer even in world literature has pursued his self-image in such various ways as Dazai.

Regardless of this uniqueness, Dazai during his youth was affected by the dominant force in Japanese fiction during the 1920's, the Proletarian School. The significance of the Proletarian School for the youthful Dazai relates more to the ideals and arguments of certain members of the school than to the generally insipid works of the proletarian writers. One argument within the school revolved about the question of whether writers from wealthy families could effectively contribute as writers to the movement. Such writers, sympathetic toward the poor and downtrodden, were ready to help. The wealthy Miyamoto Yuriko, often considered a genuine proletarian author, wrote vividly of the tenant-farmer class that was to interest Dazai. And Arishima Takeo, though commonly termed a member of the White Birch School of social humanism, composed, in "The Last Descendants of Cain," possibly the strongest indictment in Japanese fiction of the system of tenantry. Examples such as these — simply by demonstrating that writers of means did contribute to the class struggle — settle the argument for the literary and cultural historian.

But such works do not necessarily settle the question for a particular writer. Despite "The Last Descendants of Cain," Arishima Takeo came to feel in the early 1920's that, having been born into wealth, he could not become a peasant. Freeing the serfs from the farm he had inherited, Arishima declared in a famous proclamation: "I was born, raised, and educated outside the fourth class. Hence, I am one human being with no relation to the fourth class. . . . It is clearly presumptuous to think that somebody who is not a worker of the fourth class will contribute anything to the fourth class."[2] Writing sympathetically of the downtrodden was not enough for Arishima. Unable to become one of them, Arishima gave way to despair. The famous double suicide in which he and another man's wife took their lives at Karuizawa in 1923 was the ultimate consequence of that despair.

III   *The Youth of Dazai Osamu*

Like Arishima, Dazai Osamu was born into wealth. But Dazai did not wait until he was a mature man to take a critical look at undeserved fortune. With liberal and radical ideas widespread in Japan, the youthful Dazai was acutely conscious that his father's extensive landholdings and prestige were of no account. In hopes of bolstering his respect for the family, Dazai searched his genealogy for persons of worth, and he found no one. As he publicly confessed later in his life, the family had risen to prominence only when his great-grandfather managed to acquire large tracts of land in Aomori. For the idealistic Dazai, the family, despite its prosperity, had really nothing — no artist or philosopher, for example — of which it could be proud.

Probably Dazai did not know how his great-grandfather acquired so much property. If he had known he would almost certainly have written about it. In any event, Dazai hardly considered acquiring property an achievement of any merit. And, as he was well aware, the family during his own life was simply existing on the income of the land without any exertion on its part. Unimpressed by his family's wealth even as a child, Dazai later became embarrassed by and then ashamed of it.

Dazai was ten years old when he first began hearing the word "democracy." An older brother, then attending middle school in Tokyo, brought home during vacations reports on the concept as taught in the classroom. At about the same time Dazai's mother began complaining (without any real justification, apparently) that this same "democracy," in order to distribute the wealth of the country more equally, was taking year by year a larger part of the family income. Prices, according to her version of things, were constantly rising, while the family income was steadily falling.

When Dazai entered Hirosaki Higher School in 1927, he came into more direct contact with communism. Although he makes frequent reference, both in his fiction and in his autobiographical writings, to his involvement in various Communist activities, it is impossible to determine very precisely — with one or two exceptions — what Dazai did. A novel entitled *Student Comrades*, written while Dazai was still attending Hirosaki Higher School, describes a rebellion led by Communist students. According to Okuno Tateo, Dazai's description of the rebellion reflects a disturbance which did break out while Dazai was attending school.[3] Later, when he spent a number of years in Tokyo as an occasional student of French literature, Dazai was reputedly involved in many Communist plots. In autobiographical works he tells of being arrested and interrogated several times and of fleeing Tokyo once in order to escape arrest.

Nevertheless, Dazai's reputation as a Communist conspirator does not rest on solid evidence. Dazai dropped occasional hints about his activities; but these are so obscure that critics who emphasize his Communist sympathies must attribute to the author the attitudes and activities of his fictional characters. Except for distributing leaflets, Dazai did not, as far as I can determine, get involved in illegal activities of any kind.

Of course, one can always try to explain away Dazai's coyness by claiming that he did not wish to incriminate himself — even with his readers. The gap remains conspicuous, however, especially in view of the detail with which Dazai customarily recounts other parts of his life — his infancy and childhood, for example, or the pleasant days of his married life.

There is evidence for suggesting that Dazai's interest in communism expressed itself more in sympathy and identification with the cause than in specific political action. The early novel *Student Comrades* refers a number of times both to the difference between revolutionary theory and practice and to the relation of art to revolution. Writing at the high tide of the proletarian literature movement in Japan, Dazai declared that proletarian literature had proved largely ineffective in evoking political change, that the intelligentsia could produce novels and stories interesting to itself but hardly appealing to the proletariat. Aware of his own peculiar talents and his family's assets, and recalling perhaps the example of Arishima, Dazai went on to suggest that people of position, education, and authority in sympathy with the Communist movement should forget about literature as an instrument of revolution and simply lend their financial support to the cause.

Certainly Dazai doubted at times whether he could take the final step of joining actively in a conspiracy against the society represented by his own family. But he flatly rejected the ideals embodied by his family. In fact, he rejected them with barely a struggle, for he did not possess the affection for his family that would have made such a break difficult.

From the time of his earliest memories, in fact, Dazai felt himself isolated — at first from his parents and brothers, and eventually from those closest to him in childhood, his sisters and his nursemaid. At the time of Dazai's birth in 1909, his parents were already burdened with a large household. Dazai's three brothers and four sisters, his great-grandmother and grandmother, and his aunt with her four daughters all lived under one roof. The birth of Dazai's younger brother Reiji and the presence of a large entourage of servants and attendants ministering to the needs of the family increased the number of people in the house to about thirty.

Even with the best of intentions, Dazai's father and mother would have found it difficult to give love and attention to each of their children. His father, Genemon, a member of the House of Peers by virtue of the extent of his property holdings, spent most of his time in Tokyo. When on occasion he returned to Kanagi, he occupied himself receiving guests and visitors rather than cultivating relationships with his children. Dazai's mother, Tane, though seldom away from home, was in such frail health that she could neither nurse nor superintend her children. From his birth Dazai was fed by a wet nurse and disciplined by his aunt. On later occasions Dazai even claimed that he did not know which woman in the house was his mother until he was in his second or third year in school — and then only because two household servants indulged in some ill-advised teasing.

Dazai's autobiographical writings suggest that his infancy and childhood were passed almost exclusively in the company of women — his wet nurse and his aunt, his four older sisters, and a nursemaid named Take. Memories of his aunt and Take were especially vivid. His earliest memory, recorded at the very beginning of "Remembrances," concerns an attempt on the part of his aunt to instill in the infant Dazai a proper reverence for the emperor.

One evening as the sun set, I stood at the gate alongside my aunt. She was wearing her nursery coat at the time and, I believe, carried a baby on her back. She pointed at the sun silently setting in the distance and said: "The Sun, our Living God."

I remember repeating these words, but, as she scolded me and told me to address the Sun properly, I suppose I added some disrespectful remark. Then I made her laugh by asking where "our Living God" was hiding himself.[4]

Dazai's *bonne* Take was a less solemn preceptress. She often took her charge to see a painting of the Buddhist hell in a nearby temple and explained how the various punishments were in accord with the nature of the sin being punished. Dazai was horrified by a bottomless pit that sent forth white smoke. The sinners crammed into the pit, their tongues plucked, were crying out through barely opened mouths. Dazai burst into tears when Take told him this punishment was meted out to liars.

Take also taught Dazai the purpose of an odd-looking instrument behind the temple, among the wood slats with scriptural texts known as *sotoba*.

In the graveyard on a knoll behind the temple, a large cluster of *sotoba* stood alongside a hedge. In the midst of the *sotoba* there stood a black steel wheel — about the size I then imagined the full moon to be. According to Take a person turned the wheel once and let go. If the wheel did not turn back, that person would go to heaven; if it returned to its original position, the person was destined for hell.
Take would give the wheel a push, making it turn with an even sound. Invariably it stopped without turning back. But when I turned it the wheel usually returned to its starting position. I recall going alone one autumn morning to the temple. On that occasion, no matter how often I spun the wheel, fate invariably made it turn back with a clanking sound. Tired and annoyed I stubbornly pushed the wheel again and again. As evening fell I gave way to despair and left the graveyard.[5]

Throughout "Remembrances" Dazai's memories of his sisters and the household maids are more vivid than his memories of his brothers and neighborhood chums. He remembers from his infancy a frightening dream in which his aunt locked him out of the house; he recalls from his early school days how the maid Take patiently taught him to read; he looks back on adolescence as a time when he first experienced a sexual interest in such girls as his younger brother's nursemaid or the family's pert maid Miyo.

Dazai seems less interested in his brothers and schoolfellows than in his aunt or Take. He tells of them in some episodes, however. One of his older brothers, for example, brought Dazai one summer night under the mosquito netting a bag of insects at a time when Dazai was making a collection for a project at school. In general, though, Dazai, as he himself confessed, was affectionate toward his sisters and hostile toward his brothers. Again, when he describes his experiences in school, his male teachers and classmates serve primarily as an audience and sometimes as the butt of his clowning.

If one considers the early sections of the postwar novel *No Longer Human* as reflecting Dazai's personal experience as a schoolboy — and most Japanese critics do — one male character does enter Dazai's life with considerable effect. But Takeichi, the character in question, is a half idiot who sees that Yozo — the protagonist of the novel and a surrogate to some degree for the author — engages in certain antics only in order to win the laughter and recognition he craves.

Because his affections were confined during childhood mostly to the women and girls in the house, Dazai experienced at an early age the dread of loneliness that was to become a major theme in his writings. When daughters and maids in a Japanese home like Dazai's marry and go to live with their husband or their husband's family, they can lose contact with their own homes. Dazai lost his sisters one by one, and then the maid Take. Finally, even his aunt was sent to live in another place.

Reaching school age, Dazai found himself bereft of his childhood companions. Understandably, he began to acquire an oppressive consciousness of himself as an isolated individual. Applying makeup from a compact and dressing himself in a kimono, he would imitate the mincing steps of the geisha, glancing when he could at the reflection of himself in nearby mirrors and windows. On one occasion he carved a pair of lips in his desk with a penknife, painted them red, and kissed them. At the same time, Dazai was involved in sports. He particularly enjoyed long-distance running, but worked hard at it for a strange reason. He wished his dirty complexion might clear so people could not guess he had fallen into the habit of masturbating.

Early in the spring of 1923, when Dazai was preparing for the entrance examination to Aomori Middle School, news arrived from Tokyo of the death of his father. Dazai felt no grief on hearing this; indeed, he felt a secret pride that the death of his father warranted a special edition of the local newspaper. Genemon received the lavish funeral of a peer. His body, brought back to Kanagi over the snow in a sleigh, was met by crowds of people from the neighboring towns. Watching the funeral procession draw near, Dazai was entranced by the beauty of the moonlight reflecting off the hoods of the sleighs. At the funeral itself he observed only that his father appeared to be sleeping. Only when the mourners standing close by began to weep did Genemon's son cry.

During the next seven years of his schooling, first at Aomori Middle School and then at Hirosaki Higher School, Dazai struck up genuine friendships with many of his classmates. He spent weekends picnicking with his friends; he passed part of his vacations learning *gidayu*, a form of ballad chanting. When his younger brother Reiji took the entrance examination to Hirosaki Higher School, Dazai first prayed that he would fail. But when Reiji passed and came to live with Dazai, the brothers developed a genuine affection for one another. Dazai confided to Reiji his secret love for one of the maids at the house in Kanagi, and Reiji, in his turn, showed great solicitude for an acne problem bothering Dazai at the time.

In trying to understand Dazai's early development, experiences such as the foregoing must be noted. Japanese scholars of Dazai discuss these experiences, but they seem to put more weight on the vague anxieties and premonitions the young Dazai felt within himself. The following passage from one of Dazai's autobiographical writings signifies the nature of these anxieties and premonitions.

One morning, when I was a third-year student in middle school, I stopped on my way to class and leaned against the round, lacquer-stained railing of a bridge. A river about as wide as the Sumida flowed underneath, and, for several moments, I forgot myself more fully than I ever had before. Usually I would strike some pose or other in response to a feeling that someone was watching behind me. Every time I made a move, that someone would stare at his palms, scratch behind his ear, and mumble at my side. With him around, I could never act spontaneously.[6]

Then, struggling to escape this condition, Dazai catches an early glimpse of his vocation.

There were ten or twenty masks affixed to my face and I could no longer discern which was the sorrowing mask, let alone its degree of sorrow. I finally hit upon a wretched escape: writing. . . . Over and over I prayed in secret that I might become a writer.[7]

IV   *"Bottomless Abyss"*

Dazai completed only a lengthy introductory section of his first ambitious piece of writing, "Bottomless Abyss."[8] The narrative, as we have it, can best be summarized as a series of episodes detailing the emotional development of an introvert named Kanji, the young son of a well-to-do rural family in northern Japan. The first episode shows Kanji relaxing at a hot spring with his mother and sister; the second describes a pathetic attempt by a stupid servant to shock the boy by coaxing him to peek into a backyard shed at a second servant copulating with a maid. The remaining episodes principally involve the relations between Kanji, his father, and a new maid named Osada. Young and almost bereft of kin, Osada seems to Kanji unique among the household maids; while the other girls giggle at his pranks and antics, Osada simply responds with a wan smile. Osada also seems unique to Kanji's father, Shutaro. After hesitating briefly over a course of action, Shutaro establishes Osada in a separate house as his mistress. Eventually she gives birth to a child, just as certain older members of the family succeed in their attempt to pressure

Shutaro to abandon her. Osada becomes insane and Shutaro, apparently in retribution for his callousness, becomes seriously ill and dies. The narrative ends as Kanji, in the company of a friend, comes unexpectedly upon Osada's house. Though aware of Osada's insanity and his father's guilt, Kanji feels a kind of "immeasurable peace" in the presence of the house.

The plot of "Bottomless Abyss" is somewhat chaotic and melodramatic. Kanji, the center of attention almost throughout the story, seems at times something of a puzzle. Early in the narrative the boy recalls fearing that family pride in his scholastic ability might mar his future; and he recalls in addition that this fear arose just at the time he was masturbating frequently. The temptation exists to conclude that the conjunction of these two experiences points to the early stages of the boy's self-awareness. However, in accord with his customary procedure, Dazai moves quickly to other aspects of Kanji's development, leaving the passage to merely hint a meaning. Other equally perplexing passages occur, such as the final depiction of Kanji experiencing his "immeasurable peace" at the sight of Osada's house.

One could well argue that "Bottomless Abyss" is lacking in narrative continuity. Aside from their relation to Kanji's emotional development or to the environment in which that development takes place, the various episodes of the narrative have little relation to one another. There are, admittedly, a few specific continuities. For example, although Kanji despises his father, the "young master" seems on occasion a potential dictator worthy to rule the house some day. In one striking passage he rides the backs of the maids as they crawl about the floor on hands and knees. Nevertheless, the clearest indication that the events of the narrative do cohere rests on the word of the author. Dazai intrudes on several occasions, as he must, with assurances that a particular event does bear on the ultimate fate of his protagonist.

In shifting the narrative focus so readily, Dazai seems unwilling to come to terms with the significance of his material. Often he comes to the verge of developing a serious theme only to pull back. Rather than sustain an effort to probe the tragedy of such important characters as Osada, Shutaro, and (it could be argued) even Kanji, Dazai prefers to probe the tragedy of a lesser figure.

Dazai's treatment of Senko, the servant who lures Kanji to the shed for a peek at sex, illustrates the point. In a passage leading up to the sex scene, Senko first carries on an extended interior monologue.

Proud of his strength but aware of his stupidity, Senko blames himself for his inability to act decisively. During the course of the monologue his mind drifts several times between reverie and reality. The idea of inviting Kanji to the shed comes as a brainstorm. But, as Kanji peeps inside, Senko is suddenly overcome with regret. He drags the young master off into a field and breaks into a crying fit.

This memorable scene raises a number of pressing questions. "Bottomless Abyss" is narrated almost entirely from a third-person omniscient point of view. Normally Dazai simply states what a character is thinking or feeling when the need for this information arises. Why, it must be asked, is a minor figure like Senko given the privilege of revealing his mental state directly to the reader? Again, although Dazai claims at the very beginning of the scene that he intends to describe a traumatic experience that occurred to Kanji at the age of eight, he penetrates far deeper into Senko than into Kanji. Why, it must be asked, does Dazai subvert his declared intention in writing the scene?

The answers to such questions involve one in the fundamentals of Dazai's art. "Bottomless Abyss" may be an early and incomplete work, but it reveals an important clue to understanding much of Dazai's fiction. Any reader of "Bottomless Abyss" may well be forgiven the suspicion that the author is less interested in *proportioning* the role of each character in accord with the demands of theme than in securing, through any character whatever, the opportunity of voicing certain personal concerns.

In a story like "Bottomless Abyss" a specific kind of stimulus-reaction event emerges as typical. Senko, alone with the young master in a small room, must take some action to counteract his feeling of inferiority vis-à-vis both Kanji and the clever servant Kinko. Later in the story Kanji watches a woman member of an acrobatic troupe feed bananas to some monkeys. When she ignores a lone female monkey, Kanji is impelled to speak out on behalf of the monkey. In another scene Kanji finds himself at a loss with the weeping Osada. Kanji has provoked Osada's tears by asking out of the blue whether she has committed some wrong. He attempts to repair the injury wrought by his rude inquisitiveness by simply assuring Osada that she has done no wrong. Each of these scenes appears to represent a social crisis, a moment when the realization that things are out of joint impels the character to a sudden remark or action in the hope of righting the balance.

Usually the character who makes such an attempt either worsens the problem or doubts the effectiveness of his attempt. Senko, after showing Kanji the goings-on in the shed, is in a worse state than before. The woman in the acrobatic troupe turns to Kanji with a simple explanation: "She is ill." As he tries to console the weeping Osada, Kanji feels that he's encountered a like scene and wonders whether Osada doesn't have a similar feeling. In their relations with others, then, people try to redress appearances of inferiority, of wrong, of guilt. But the attempt simply creates a second mishap; there seems no way to right the balance. The title, which designates one of the numerous Buddhist hells, underlines the pessimistic character of the tale. "Bottomless Abyss" is the first of a considerable line of moral dilemmas Dazai spun about his characters (and himself).

V *"Those Two and Their Pathetic Mother"*

Like "Bottomless Abyss," "Those Two and Their Pathetic Mother" is concerned with moments of social crisis; the latter story, however, treats this problem solely within the confines of one family. There are additional differences to be noted. In "Bottomless Abyss" the household is large and wealthy, and the crucial familial relationship is that between Kanji and his father; in "Those Two and Their Pathetic Mother" the family seems relatively poor and the only familial relationships at all are those among a mother and her two sons. Furthermore, in "Those Two and Their Pathetic Mother" Dazai comes to grips with a question he ignored in "Bottomless Abyss," namely, whether the family can function as a unit.

"Those Two and Their Pathetic Mother" describes how the mother and her younger son, Ryuji, come from their village in the northern part of Japan to visit the older son, Koichiro, in Tokyo. Earlier, the entire family lived in Tokyo, where the father was a government official; but, with the death of the father, the mother has returned with Ryuji to her native village, reluctantly leaving behind the son who insisted on remaining to pursue a career as a sculptor.

When he and his mother reach the capital, Ryuji begins to regret his insistence that the trip be made. For one thing, a kidney ailment troubling Koichiro appears a matter of inconvenience rather than serious concern. Again, arriving at the station, Ryuji is totally ignored by his mother, who, in response to the disdain with which her younger boy has treated her on the train, attaches herself firmly to Koichiro. Finally, the arrogant Koichiro treats Ryuji with all the superiority and hauteur he can muster as the older and more experienced brother.

During the stay at Koichiro's house Ryuji and his mother idle away their time while Koichiro complains that their presence is more a hindrance to his art than consolation in his illness. There are a few moments of warmth. When Ryuji himself falls briefly ill with stomach trouble, his mother and Koichiro minister to him with patience and care. When Koichiro finishes an important segment of a work of sculpture, he invites his mother and brother to dine in a department-store restaurant. But these occasions are few and seem to occur almost by accident. In the final sentences of the story Dazai describes how Ryuji suddenly understands his mother's reason for visiting Tokyo.

Ryuji suddenly looked up and saw his haggard mother being jostled in the midst of a crowd of shoppers. He recognized in her the shadow of old age and death and, in that moment, everything became clear to him. He understood why his mother had come to Tokyo so impulsively and why she did not wish to return home.
Koichiro was standing before the elevator motioning to them.
Together the three of them entered the dim cage. The heavy metal grillwork clanged shut and the elevator began to ascend.[9]

Despite their antagonisms the three occupants of the elevator are bound together by a force much stronger than their individual feelings. Symbolic passages are not common in Dazai's works, and the foregoing description is all the more powerful for that reason.

The entire narrative of "Those Two and Their Pathetic Mother" is held within the confines of the title. To a degree Dazai seems intent on showing how this particular set of individuals cannot function as a family except under extraordinary circumstances or under fiat. But the author seems even more intent on examining a related question, that is, the way in which changing circumstances drastically alter the expectations of and relations among the members of a family.

The following interpretation of "Those Two and Their Pathetic Mother" draws together many parts of the narrative. Ryuji urges the visit to Tokyo, but suffers the most from the experience. He acts coldly toward his uncouth mother on the train only to feel bereft when she offers her affection to Koichiro at the station in Tokyo. The conservative mother, disturbed by Koichiro's unconventional habits, hopes that Ryuji will pursue a traditional career in the manner of her dead husband. Yet, given the truth of Ryuji's intuition in the final scene, she is aware that her own death is imminent and is anxious, therefore, to remain with the son she doesn't understand. Having ignored his mother on the train in smug awareness of his cultural superiority, Ryuji is in turn put to shame in a variety of ways by the smug Koichiro. The narrative is replete with descriptions of superior-inferior relations of status and intelligence, relations that disappear only momentarily when an illness calls forth a response of sympathy and generosity.

Dazai had to pay a price for exercising such ironic control. In comparison to "Bottomless Abyss," "Those Two and Their Pathetic Mother" is a tame tale woefully lacking the lively style and startling turns of plot evident in the earlier story. In "Bottomless Abyss" (and, to anticipate, in most of Dazai's later work too) there is at certain moments a quaintness of language and eccentricity of style immediately recognizable to the informed reader as uniquely Dazai's. For instance, Dazai often uses a mildly "prissy" effeminate manner to describe men and women anxious about their appearance. In "Bottomless Abyss" Osada, responding to a summons from Shutaro, is described in the following manner:

She had just begun plying her needle when she heard the chiming bell summoning her to the master's room. She let the Oshima quilt slide from her knees as she rose and picked the bits of thread from her apron one by one. Adjusting her kimono in front with care, she blithely hastened toward the master's room.[10]

In "Those Two and Their Pathetic Mother" the "effeminant tone" echoes faintly in a brief passage describing Koichiro as he sits on the edge of his bed "stroking his long shining hair."

In "Those Two and Their Pathetic Mother" Dazai tries his hand at comedy a number of times, comedy which, viewed in retrospect from the point of view of the later Dazai, seems rather out of character.

The waiter brought the dinner menu from the dining car. Mother took and examined it carefully, even though she couldn't read. Look! Look! She's got it upside down!
"You've got it upside down, Mother."[11]

Once he lay down Ryuji felt almost laughably weak. His older brother brought tears into Ryuji's eyes as he said: "Shall we put you in my bed?" No longer did Ryuji feel contempt for his mother; indeed he felt apologetic toward her and Koichiro. His worry that the money his mother brought would be wasted on his illness was in vain. His mind was as empty as his stomach.[12]

His was a hard life, utterly without vision, and Ryuji was tired of it. Whatever he tried seemed dreary. Once he bought a book on *How to Improve the Outhouse Toilet* and made an earnest study of the problem.[13]

Admittedly the English renderings are unfair to Dazai. Considerable allowance must be made for humorous possibilities in Japanese (especially of a mild scatological kind) which cannot be carried over into English. And yet, though the Japanese of Dazai is less drab than the English used to translate him here, the original conveys almost as transparently as the translation the hopelessness of Dazai's attempt to be funny.

Dazai, it would appear, had not yet mastered the mechanism by which he attempts humor in "Those Two and Their Pathetic Mother." As we shall see, most of his better humorous effects at this stage of his career are achieved through upsetting expectations and hopes. Instead of patiently laying out situations which permit such types of humor, Dazai in "Those Two and Their Pathetic Mother" thrusts here and there into the narrative a sentence or brief paragraph intended to be witty in itself. Judged by his performance Dazai does not seem at this point to command the swift, adept wit necessary to effect this kind of humor.

To some extent Dazai's focus on the family in "Those Two and Their Pathetic Mother" resulted in a style and manner quite distinct from the earlier story "Bottomless Abyss." Such a view of "Those Two and Their Pathetic Mother" is incomplete, however. Ryuji is shown as he functions within the family, but the detail with which he is portrayed makes him a markedly more individual study than either the mother or Koichiro. To a degree Ryuji is a continuation of Kanji, granted the differences in character and circumstance — the fact, for example, that Ryuji has slightly foppish pretensions in spite of his ugliness while Kanji has none, or that Ryuji seems less obsessed than Kanji with the burden of the family past. Certain passages — the mother's notion that Ryuji resembles his father, a hint in the description of the train ride that Ryuji's dour attitude is in contrast to his normal comic spirit — impart to the reader the definite impression that Ryuji is Kanji in a new guise. Indeed, the necessity of linking the two boys in some fashion becomes apparent as one moves on to later Dazai stories. Dazai often creates as his central figure a character wholly understandable only to the reader aware of the prototypes in the earlier fiction.

The reason for this state of affairs is simple: Dazai is more fascinated by himself than by his characters. In understanding Dazai, the individual characters in a given work are less significant than certain "archetypal" experiences that occur to a variety of characters in different works and that seem crucially personal to the author. In "Bottomless Abyss" the crucial experiences belong principally to Kanji and Senko; secondarily they belong to Shutaro and Osada. In "Those Two and Their Pathetic Mother" Ryuji alone undergoes a "crucial" experience. Ryuji is disconsolate in the realization that, in comparison to Koichiro, he is ugly and weak-willed; he is embarrassed over his inability to grasp things quickly and act decisively. In the context of Dazai's family scheme, Ryuji is the successor to Kanji; in his psychic dimension, however, he inherits the problems of the servant Senko.

In limiting himself in "Those Two and Their Pathetic Mother" to Ryuji alone as the vehicle for voicing the personal concerns conveyed through several characters in "Bottomless Abyss," Dazai adopted a manner of presentation and a style less free than those employed in the earlier story. He was, I would argue, less comfortable with the mode of "Those Two and Their Pathetic Mother" than with the freer style of "Bottomless Abyss." Probably he intended the story as a thematically complete work brought to its conclusion by a symbolic scene. But the resolution of "Those Two and Their Pathetic Mother" in a passage showing the members of the family trapped with one another is arbitrary. The story does not resolve itself; Dazai simply brings it to an end.

VI *"Landlord for a Generation"*

"Bottomless Abyss" and "Those Two and Their Pathetic Mother" contain passages which directly reflect the thoughts and feelings of a given character. In "Landlord for a Generation" Dazai wrote for the first time an extended story told in full from the first-person point of view. Curiously, the character he created as his initial first-person narrator appears to a considerable extent beyond the favor and sympathy of the author.

The narrator is the landlord of the story title, a man who appears to be in his twenties. He begins by referring to certain accounts and rumors of a rift between himself and his tenant farmers. The landlord claims the facts have been distorted and that he hopes, through his own account, to put the record straight. As he begins writing down the facts as he sees them, his younger brother enters the room. This provides the landlord with the occasion to speak of his ambition to become a writer. He shows his brother a sample of writing recently accepted for newspaper publication — a bizarre autobiographical account of childhood memories which includes several faintly erotic scenes.

Returning after this diversion to his original purpose, the landlord relates several events that have turned his younger brother and himself into bitter enemies. A year earlier, with the landlord in bed with a severe case of venereal disease, a pretty young nurse named Segawa had come to the house. According to the landlord, his brother, who had never liked him, came to visit the sickroom daily — merely to see Segawa. The landlord claims that Segawa was attracted to him and that he eventually seduced her. Shortly thereafter Segawa became fatally ill with venereal disease. To avenge her the younger brother has spread rumors in the neighborhood that the landlord is responsible for her death.

A second dispute between the brothers involves the older brother's conduct as landlord. After doubling the farmers' rent on somewhat specious grounds, the landlord tries to reclaim from the tenants a piece of land to build a tennis court. The tenants offer a compromise. This the landlord refuses; to back up his claim, he calls in the police to arrest several of the tenant negotiators. The resort to force enrages the tenants and they begin laying plans for a revolt.

The final events described by the landlord take place during the night preceding the anticipated attack on his house. With the home fortified, and police and military on alert, the landlord ascends to his roof in the dark. Presently his brother comes up, and the two fall to arguing about political and ideological matters, the younger brother taking the part of the oppressed tenants. Eventually they move to an underground chamber and finally, for a discussion with their mother, to a room housing the family's Buddhist shrine. Appalled at the audacity of the tenants, the conservative mother counsels that the family hold its ground for the honor of its ancestors. The story ends with the brothers still at odds, but relieved that the dawn will bring forth a battle to determine which side owns the future.

Dazai's use of first-person narration raises several questions. Admittedly the landlord shows himself a "reliable narrator" in Wayne Booth's sense of the term.[14] The reader has no doubt as to the basic facts surrounding Segawa's death and the tenant dispute. True, the landlord is a prejudiced participant in the events, but his prejudice is so extreme that he merely arrogates the justice in each case entirely to his own point of view. Self-righteousness as narrow as his does not conceive the possibility or advisability of doctoring the facts.

The question naturally arises: to whom is he addressing himself? The text of his account contains few clues. Since the landlord is at first concerned with rectifying distorted accounts circulated by rumor and the newspapers, it would seem that he intends his account for the public at large, or perhaps for the educated public.

I suspect, however, that Dazai, at this stage of his development, was not concerned with such technical matters as the implied audience of his first-person narrations. It would be difficult even to argue that he is concerned with the quality of mind inherent in the manner in which the landlord spins his tale. The manner in which Dazai chanced to unfold "Landlord for a Generation" opened the way for interesting literary effects. The landlord is recalling the past, and describing that past to an unspecified audience, in order to justify his own position and behavior. Reviewing the past, he tends to dramatize his own role and relive the emotions he once felt. Yet Dazai seems far more interested in providing the reader with the comedy of the landlord figure than in probing the psychological truth of a character caught in such a peculiar situation.

Few readers could get very far into "Landlord for a Generation" without coming to regard the narrator as a fool. At times Dazai goes out of his way to make the man an insufferable boor. The landlord insistently claims for himself virtues he obviously lacks. He shows to his brother the autobiographical fragment of his childhood, proud that this work has been accepted for publication. But the work turns out to be unbelievably haphazard and fatuous. He thinks himself courageous, but must constantly remember to act courageously as he confronts the angry tenants. He harps on his own authority as master vis-à-vis the "slaves" who work within his domain; yet he expresses pride in his status most specifically when he points to the fifty-mat size of the family parlor (a room of approximately nine-hundred square feet).

Nevertheless, Dazai holds back from portraying the landlord as a complete villain and fool. A reader aware of Dazai's values will recognize some faint signs of sympathy on the part of the author. The landlord wishes to write partly out of a sense of fun. Alone with his brother on the roof, he confesses his responsibility for Segawa's death. Even as he commits his most savage act, poisoning a pond full of carp which have been carefully nurtured by an old tenant, the landlord confesses to a "rotten feeling."

Admittedly these are trifles alongside the overbearing arrogance and evil of the man. However, there is one far more important way in which the landlord emerges as a figure of sympathy — not so much within the story itself as within the context of Dazai's emerging view of man. Prior to "Landlord for a Generation" Dazai's most significant characters were younger sons, still undergoing the trials of adolescent self-consciousness. In his humanity, as opposed to his status, the landlord is afflicted by many of the problems and inadequacies of the younger-son figures. Like Ryuji, the landlord is clumsy in his movements and rash in his social reactions; like Kanji, he is oppressed by family ways and traditions. However, in his pride and stupidity, the landlord, for the most part, is blissfully unaware of his limitations. Had he followed his normal practice, Dazai would have shown the landlord as oversensitive and painfully self-conscious. He shows instead a landlord making empty gestures, appealing to a fading authority and mistaken image of himself. Surely Dazai felt pity for a man who understood himself no better than the landlord did.

In examining other figures in "Landlord for a Generation," allowance must be made for the fact that Dazai uses these characters primarily as a means of provoking in the landlord those reactions he wishes to display for his readers. So great are the social prejudices of the landlord that he doesn't feel the need to alter the reality of other people and other social classes in the story. Thus, although the reader's view of characters other than the landlord is indirect, it is nevertheless accurate.

The briefly treated younger brother in "Landlord for a Generation" is especially intriguing for readers of "Bottomless Abyss" and "Those Two and Their Pathetic Mother." In "Landlord for a Generation" the older brother reports on several confrontations with the younger, most significantly, the final dramatic meeting that begins on the roof of the family house. Although the landlord despises his brother for both his politics and his interference in the Segawa affair, he represents him as confident and clever. In one confrontation with the farmers, the landlord loses his poise when one of the men suddenly identifies himself as the brother of Segawa. Later the landlord discovers — and duly reports to readers of his narrative — that the man was a counterfeit enlisted by his wily brother to aid the farmers. Again, the younger brother always appears to know far more than the landlord about what is brewing among the tenants; indeed, he comes to personify for his brother the threat of an overthrow of traditional authority.

Occasionally, one of the tenant farmers, the supposed brother of Segawa, for example, or the old man who patiently tends the carp, emerges briefly as an individual. Generally, however, Dazai treats the tenants as a group. The landlord does not see them as people; for him they are a massed threat which must be overcome.

Nevertheless, Dazai takes care to show the virtues of the tenant class. Aware of the injustice in the landlord's attempt to reappropriate land for a tennis court, the farmers are still willing to allow him his legal rights. But, in recognition of the hardships which would arise for one of them in an immediate transfer, the farmers plead that the transfer of land be delayed a year. In contrast to the willingness and flexibility of the farmers, the landlord shows himself to be rigid and callous. In one of his most fatuous moments he responds: "If I don't get the court built now, the snow will fall and I'll have to wait till it melts."

Also, in contrast to the family with its violent split between the brothers and ineffectual appeal for unity by the mother, the farmers show a splendid esprit de corps. Dazai describes them as sympathetic to each other and ready to take action to avenge a wrong done to any one of them. The landlord, poised on his roof alone in the dark, becomes a doubly forlorn figure as he watches the silhouettes of peasants moving together about the fires in their distant camp.

Unfortunately, Dazai does not deal seriously with the younger brother's relation to the tenants. The youngster does seize a brief chance to blurt out a few words in the final scene during an argument with the landlord:

"The workers are strong. Whether farmers or laborers they've got a grip on everything in the world. No matter how much you wave your sword, brother, it won't do you a bit of good. You know the joke about the hunter who climbs a whale's back mistaking it for an island and shouts for a whale to appear. We're all dancing on the whale's back, that's for certain. The only question is whether or not the whale's aware of us."[15]

A colorful expression of Marxism, surely, but one which sheds little light on the younger brother's understanding of the peasants, or his grasp of the nature and consequences of rebellion.

VII   Student Comrades

In his next lengthy story, *Student Comrades*, Dazai again took up the theme of rebellion. The rebellion in *Student Comrades* is based in the main on an episode that occurred at the Hirosaki Higher School while Dazai was a student there. When the principal was accused of embezzling from a student fund, a large part of the student body clamored for a strike; another group of students counseled moderation, while the faculty found itself, as usual, caught between the conflicting demands of conservative administrators and radical, voluble students. In an attempt to reveal various aspects of the disturbance, Dazai found himself dealing with a larger group of characters and a more complex set of personal relationships than in any earlier work. With the rebellion and movements of student factions in the forefront, there is little room in *Student Comrades* for scenes of private brooding.

The narrative consists primarily of a series of episodes in which the factions attempt either to promote or thwart the strike. When the story opens, the embezzlement has occurred and the students assembled to discuss a course of action are splitting into two groups, one lenient toward the principal, the other calling for strong action by the student body. When the principal suddenly appears in the assembly hall and begins an apology, pandemonium breaks out.

The remainder of the narrative alternates between the two student factions with their plots and counterplots. There are several vivid scenes showing the attempt of a group to determine consensus and mobilize for action. More commonly a scene is restricted to an exchange between a pair of students, usually those belonging to the radical faction. Aside from their alliance to the same faction, the two students in a given scene are characteristically shown in contrast to one another. Hosoya believes the principal's resignation and return of the embezzled money will satisfy the demands of justice; his friend Kijima, however, holds out for *seppuku*. Yamazaki, the son of a farmer, warns his wealthy friend Yoshino that the unrest is mere "heroic posturing" by a radical elite. Aoi distinguishes himself from his companion, Kobayakawa, and the rest of the students favoring a strike by calling himself a "bourgeois" and the others "petit bourgeois."

The alternation of scenes between the two maneuvering factions arouses a degree of curiosity as to which side will win. Instead of satisfying this curiosity, however, Dazai directs his attention, in the final scene, to the principal. He is at home making preparations to move elsewhere in the wake of his resignation. He first hears the servants boldly arguing about his "crime" as they pack luggage in a nearby room, then suffers an even greater indignity with the realization that his own son is outside in the dark aiding an attempt by radical students to keep the house under surveillance. This scene brings the story to an overly abrupt end, as critics generally favorable to Dazai are willing to admit.

The contrastive pairing of characters in most of the scenes is underlined by additional techniques. Dazai shows various sides of the same person by pairing him with different characters in different scenes. Further, he differentiates a radical set of students from a representative of the conservative group at one point within an obvious narrative trick. The radical students are talking to one another when the conservative unexpectedly appears. Having shifted the attention of the radical pair to this opponent as he goes past and disappears, Dazai deliberately lets the narrative remain focused on the conservative as he proceeds on his business.

Such techniques of "grouping" and "linking," in conjunction with the polemical subject matter, seem appropriate to a story that develops in dialectic fashion. Within the basic dichotomy of the two student factions, *Student Comrades* generates a conflict of subordinate ideas and attitudes sufficient to sustain in the reader a considerable forensic interest. The gap between theory and reality is forcibly conveyed in Yoshino's visit to the lumberyard owned by his father. Yoshino has read of merciless oppression and of just anger in proletarian novels; but the laborers under his father seem blissfully ignorant and content. As we have seen, Yamazaki, though himself a radical, castigates the radical group for its elitism.

These attempts to qualify ideology were hardly meant, it seems to me, to turn the story into an intellectual search for a definition. Rather than help forward a polemical story to its resolution, the concern for qualifying reveals the ironic turn of mind characteristic of Dazai. The ending of *Student Comrades*, with the principal suddenly aware of his son's betrayal, makes some sense as an autobiographically inspired statement of the author's ironic view of things. In relation to the polemic terms of the story, the final scene makes no sense whatever.

In *Student Comrades* Dazai demonstrates again his ability to quickly sketch scenes of startling visual impact. A student named Takimitsu, who recalls the adolescent Dazai in his physical appearance, emerges several times as an eerie figure. On one occasion he emerges foul of breath from a café and weaves his way into the thick evening fog; in another scene he comes upon his friends one night after getting slapped by his pregnant mistress, a line of black blood running down his cheek "like silk thread." Several comic passages are notably visual. Aware that the meek Instructor Sasayama enjoys the patronage of the principal, a student amuses himself with the image of Sasayama's dwarfish body sprawled on the floor of a geisha house, his head pillowed on the knees of a pretty attendant.

In stories prior to *Student Comrades* Dazai seemed to be using the younger son as the main vehicle for conveying his own attitudes and moods. While Takimitsu seems like Dazai in appearance, Aoi, the son of a wealthy rural landlord, appears to serve as the author's alter ego. Aoi plays a significant part in the story only once, in a section entitled "The Vanquished" which describes a lengthy conversation between himself and a radical student named Kobayakawa. Aoi calls to mind the younger sons of the earlier stories: his father, like Kanji's, has died of consumption; like the younger brother of "Landlord for a Generation" Aoi has allied himself with a rebellion by tenant farmers against the rule of his own family. Older than either of the boys in the earlier stories, Aoi has known certain fears still latent in Kanji or the younger brother of "Landlord for a Generation." Aoi fears he has inherited the tendency toward consumption that killed his father, and he has attempted suicide after the failure of the rebellion.

In his conversation with Kobayakawa, Aoi reveals a sense of isolation that stands in sharp contrast to the camaraderie shared by the other students. *Student Comrades* consists by and large of descriptions of how groups function and exert power, and the most lyrical passage in the work celebrates the warmth and esprit de corps felt by the radical students in the presence of each other.

Aoi despairs of ever being able to join the endeavors of his fellows. He tells Kobayakawa that he is a bourgeois and the others petit bourgeois. He claims he has inherited from his father an impulse toward dissipation that disqualifies him from undertaking such serious pursuits as revolution. A strenuous effort to purge himself of this base nature has merely shown that his instinctual heritage is stronger than his will. He ventures the notion that people like himself are "less than human" and deserve death.

Ironically, this sudden confession of failure brings an intense response of friendship from Kobayakawa. Assuring Aoi of his friendship, Kobayakawa begs him not to die. Then Kobayakawa departs for a meeting in tears, leaving Aoi his "infinite love and solicitude and shrieking his determination to succeed as he descends the stairs of the boarding house."

The scene, then, ends in farce. The reader pictures Aoi left behind in the room shaking his head in disbelief. Kobayakawa, even with the best of intentions, could hardly bring consolation to Aoi. Indeed, there are good reasons for arguing that Aoi prefers his alienation. He seems to take considerable pride in viewing himself as an outsider with problems and agonies beyond the understanding of his fellow students. He regards himself as so singled out by fate that no degree of resolve and effort can change him.

Aoi again reveals his proud isolation in the rationale he has developed as an aspiring writer. In a series of remarks that echo Dazai, Aoi condemns the proletarian literature movement in Japan as irrelevant to genuine social and political problems. If the intelligentsia wish to support rebellion, they should write bourgeois novels and donate the royalties to radical causes. For himself, however, Aoi has found a more antisocial motive for writing.

People who write poems and novels which aren't read and don't make money, who write as a form of masturbation, are the most content. In the act of writing, various phantasies come to mind and one comes eventually to feel ineffably good, as if he's performing mankind's most splendid act. Literature as opiate. And when it becomes a habit, it's no use for other people to moralize. You don't quit a thing like masturbating.[16]

VIII   *The Period of Apprenticeship*

Critical studies of Dazai Osamu customarily begin with his first major collection of stories and sketches, entitled *Final Years*. The works covered in the present chapter at best receive brief mention; usually they are ignored.

Dazai, still a student in higher school, was experimenting with various plots and styles. Later in his career he repeatedly confessed to ineptitude at organizing a story. During this period of apprenticeship, he often seems to order the events of his story in an arbitrary manner, the sudden shift in focus to the principal at the end of *Student Comrades* being one obvious example. Perhaps Dazai himself sensed the clumsiness in his handling of certain plots; the suggestion has been advanced that he left both *Student Comrades* and "Landlord for a Generation" in an unfinished state.

It is quite possible that Dazai was looking to other literary works for plot suggestions. Going through Japanese proletarian literature, for example, one comes upon several works that might have been in Dazai's mind, consciously or unconsciously, as he composed "Landlord for a Generation." In Kaneko Yobun's *Hell*, published in 1923, a rural landlord of great wealth and power is depicted. Like the older brother in "Landlord for a Generation," the landlord Sakata brutally repulses a group of tenant farmers who present him with a perfectly reasonable petition, in this instance a petition relating to a severe drought. Like the elder brother of "Landlord for a Generation," Sakata has inherited his estate; again like the brother, Sakata is very lustful and utterly callous in acting out his lust.

The theme of the landlord's son sympathizing with the tenants was also used by proletarian writers. A story entitled "Landlord," written in 1923 by Fujimori Seikichi, depicts a young aspiring writer named Koyama. Living in the city, Koyama is not directly affected by the tenant-farmer disturbance in "Landlord." Nevertheless, he tries to adjust his life in the city in ways he imagines will help ameliorate the sufferings of the tenants. More important, as a landlord's son and aspiring writer, he wishes to make a contribution by writing about the social problems of the tenant farmer.

Japanese critics and scholars have not attempted to gauge the degree of Dazai's indebtedness for plot suggestions to such works as *Hell* and "Landlord," perhaps because of the general nature of the similarities mentioned above. Surely one claim is admissible, however; if Dazai was borrowing, his practice here differs from what it became later in his career when he unabashedly took over plots from such diverse sources as *Hamlet* and Schiller's *Die Burgschaft*. By then, Dazai, confident of his own comic style, could turn such works upside down and make them his own.

Presumably Dazai was open to the influence of various writing styles during this period of apprenticeship. Although Japanese critics and scholars are not agreed on specific influences, it seems that apparently detectable influences are really just temporarily "borrowed styles," which, being in some way unsuitable, did not become a permanent part of Dazai's style, already basically formed as humorous self-caricature. However, this is to jump to a conclusion. A reader going through Dazai's works chronologically will recognize the humor; but at this point he does not know Dazai well enough to realize that such humor is meant as self-caricature. That realization comes only with reading the later, more mature works.

CHAPTER 2

The Period of Final Years
(1930-1935)

I *The Biography*

DAZAI Osamu moved to Tokyo in April, 1930, ostensibly to study French literature at Tokyo Imperial University. He first rented a room in Totsuka, just a few blocks from the lodging of an older brother then studying sculpture. Three months after Dazai's arrival, however, the brother fell ill and died. In "Eight Views of Tokyo," an autobiographical account of this period published in 1941, Dazai refers to his brother's death and adds: "From the second semester [i.e., according to the Japanese academic calendar, from September] I quit going to the university almost entirely."[1]

Soon Dazai found himself with another companion from home. Koyama Hatsuyo, a young geisha he had known since his days at the Hirosaki Higher School, arrived one autumn afternoon at Dazai's room. His description of the incident does not suggest any affection on his part for Hatsuyo. Yet when his oldest brother hastened to Tokyo to prevent a scandal, Dazai insisted, before releasing Hatsuyo, that he be allowed to marry her eventually.

Left alone in Tokyo, Dazai grew despondent. Back in Aomori, Hatsuyo, who would prove a fickle creature on subsequent occasions, did not answer Dazai's letters, though she was entirely free to do so. Furthermore, Dazai learned that, despite his brother's promise, the family did not look with favor on the "engagement" of one of its members — particularly a Tokyo University student — to a local geisha.

Dazai claimed in "Eight Views of Tokyo" that the family's disapproval of Hatsuyo drove him to attempt suicide.[2] One November evening in 1930, after only a half year's residence in Tokyo, Dazai journeyed to the beach at Kamakura in the company of a hostess from a Ginza bar. There he and the hostess attempted to drown themselves together in the sea. The woman was lost, but Dazai survived. The police, after seizing Dazai as an accomplice to a suicide, were about to press charges when the author's brother arrived from home just in time to intervene — much to the relief of the family. When the brother returned to Kanagi, he granted Hatsuyo permission to go to live with Dazai in Tokyo.

Too restless to remain very long content with any situation, Dazai soon found new cause for despair. Describing Hatsuyo's arrival in Tokyo in the autobiographical "Eight Views of Tokyo," Dazai mentions her "innocence" and stresses that, despite having known one another for several years, they had never become lovers. Afterward, reading one evening in Rousseau's *Confessions* how the author tried to uncover his wife's past, Dazai felt tempted to put Hatsuyo to the test. By insistent questioning he discovered to his dismay that Hatsuyo was not so innocent and inexperienced as he had imagined.

After he had passed two years in Tokyo, Dazai had troubles other than with Hatsuyo. He was involved in enough left-wing activity to imagine that the police would like to get their hands on him. If in truth they had considered him a danger, Dazai would no doubt have grown in self-respect and pride. But when he turned himself over to the police in a particularly despondent moment, they immediately released him. Again, finding himself in the police station on another occasion, Dazai was released on the grounds that an ineffectual person such as he seemed to be could not have helped a revolution even with the best of intentions.[3] On such occasions Dazai no doubt experienced the isolation of the outsider disqualified from joining the game — an emotion constantly found in his early work *Student Comrades*.

Neglecting his work at the university brought additional worries to Dazai. Instead of admitting that he had lost interest in his studies, Dazai allowed his family to think that he was faithfully attending classes. His oldest brother, the head of the family, continued to send Dazai a monthly allowance adequate to support both the author and Hatsuyo. Dazai accepted the money under the pretense that he was working for a degree. When the year of his expected graduation passed, Dazai asked his brother for an additional year. And when that year elapsed, Dazai was given a second year of grace. Apparently, Dazai deceived others besides his family. During the time he was enrolled at Tokyo University, he left his room each morning dressed in the conventional dark uniform of the Japanese university student. Hatsuyo, living with Dazai from the first year of his stay in Tokyo, evidently never thought to question his sincerity of purpose.

With a little determination Dazai could have extricated himself from the situation. The best Japanese universities, then as well as now, were difficult to enter; but, once the candidate had passed the entrance examination and enrolled in a department, he was almost assured of graduating. Dazai once described how a friend took him to the university for an interview with a certain professor of French. The professor told Dazai he would make the degree examination absurdly easy. Assured of a degree, Dazai, who often deliberately courted trouble for himself, failed to appear for the examination.

In his later writings, when he assumed the role of the moralist, Dazai confessed to much personal vice; but he declared that, unlike many of his countrymen, he had never been a hypocrite. Perhaps he saw that, by accepting a degree under such circumstances, he would appear to value something he considered worthless merely to satisfy the expectations of his family.

At any rate, he had been pursuing a project satisfying to himself and capable of mollifying the family in its inevitable disappointment over his academic failure. The story is a familiar one within Japanese literary circles. Convinced that he could not make a success of his life, Dazai determined to attempt suicide once again. But, wishing to leave a testament, he began what he considered an unvarnished account of the important experiences of his life — from the earliest moments he could recall. Dazai thought of this work, "Remembrances," as "posthumous," as the "first act" of a drama that contained no "second act." But, having finished "Remembrances," he was unwilling to quit. Sensing that he had left something unsaid, he tried his hand at one story, then another — never completely satisfied with the result. The sudden compulsion, Dazai said, was a "demon . . . devouring" him, forcing him to write.[4]

In the course of several years, Dazai collected the stories as they accumulated in a paper bag in the closet. When he had written twenty-one works he selected the fourteen he considered best and threw the remaining manuscripts in a fire in his backyard. Hatsuyo, who watched Dazai burn the manuscripts, was aghast at the nonchalance with which he could destroy what had cost him so much time and effort to produce.

For the next four years, from 1933 to 1936, Dazai gave his manuscripts one by one, as the need for money arose, to friends in a position to have them published. Later they were collected and published as *Final Years*, a title reflecting Dazai's intention at the time of writing to take his life. When Dazai first published these works, he hoped to convince his brother — who himself had on occasion written for local magazines during his student days — that, despite his academic failure, he had not simply frittered away his time in Tokyo.

II *"Leaves"*

"Leaves," the earliest work by Dazai available in English translation, is a montage of comment, anecdote, and incident. Certain sections, notably the description of the lascivious grandmother of "Landlord for a Generation," quote passages from earlier published works; other parts are purportedly taken from the stories Dazai abandoned.

Although he retouched certain passages quoted from earlier works, Dazai did not attempt, in the manner of Raymond Queneau, to create different versions of the same incident. Indeed, "Leaves" is the sort of work that tempts one to agree with Edward Seidensticker's complaint about Dazai's morbid preoccupation with what he had already written.

Given the random character of "Leaves," it appears justifiable to offer, in place of a summary, a selection of a few of the more striking passages.

For the first time in his life he held an arithmetic text in his hands. A small volume, bound in black, an impressive array of figures inside. The boy fumbled the book awhile, then discovered all the answers at the back. He frowned. "Insulting!"[5]

A full moon. Shining, collapsing, rising, falling, waves coiling and turning, her hand clinging to mine, desperate, I broke free and suddenly she was engulfed crying a name. It wasn't my name.[6]

One morning, as I was frying sardines, I heard a stray cat meowing in the garden. I went to the veranda. "Psit." The cat rose and came toward me slowly. I threw a sardine. She ate, her body tensed to flee any moment. Moved by this acceptance I stepped down to the garden to stroke her white fur. Just as I touched her back, the cat bit the middle of my little finger to the bone.[7]

He spent three full years trying to educate his wife. By the time her education was complete, he had begun to wish he were dead.[8]

The beauty of art, that is to say, the beauty of serving people.[9]

Carve on the stone pedestal the following inscription: "Here stands a man. He was born, died, and spent a life destroying his ill-written manuscripts.[10]

III *"Remembrances"*

Dazai, it will be recalled, began writing "Remembrances" as a testament to his own life. Reading the work, one can readily discern the pessimism incessantly turning the author's thoughts toward suicide; at the same time one can also detect the creative energy that impelled Dazai to go on composing, after he finished "Remembrances," the remaining works in *Final Years.*

"Remembrances" displays the swift turns of event and quick surprises evident in the earlier works. At the same time it reveals an author more attentive than before to problems of organization and transition. Composed of two contrasting parts, the memoir treats first Dazai's infancy and childhood and then his adolescence. The author's entry into middle school at the age of fourteen divides the two periods chronologically. In thematic terms, infancy and childhood are characterized by affection and contentment while adolescence is a time of trouble and anxious searching for friendship.

Even the small syntatical units of "Remembrances" show evidence of Dazai's concern for balance and completeness. Claiming that he was ugly while the youngest of his older brothers and his sole younger brother were both handsome, Dazai writes of an unbearable pressure on him from both above and below. Having spoken in one passage of his feelings toward his father, he logically moves on to his feelings toward his mother. Once on the subject of the women in the house, he is impelled to write accounts of all his sisters as well as his grandmother and aunt.

Along with this wider range of personalities and greater span of time than was usual for him at this stage, Dazai experimented with different styles of writing. Describing events of his infancy he sometimes uses a laconic style which gives the impression that parts of the biography have escaped his memory. In recounting other events, however, he is exact and detailed. For example, the incident of turning the "wheel of fate" in a temple graveyard quoted in chapter one is introduced in the following manner.

Take taught me ethics. Often she took me to the temple to explain the paintings of heaven and hell. The arsonists were made to carry flaming baskets, men who had kept a mistress struggled in the coils of a green two-headed snake. Pale, meager figures crying out through barely opened mouths filled certain regions: the pond of blood, the mountain of needles, the bottomless pit filled with white smoke.[11]

Dazai's use of a laconic style raises a crucial question about his intentions in writing "Remembrances." After describing a fearful en-

counter with his father, Dazai proceeds to describe his relation to his
mother.

> I felt no love for my mother either. Nursed by a maid, caressed by a
> aunt, I didn't even realize who my mother was until my second or third year
> of grade school. In fact, two male servants taught me that.
> One night my mother, resting nearby, grew suspicious of the way my quilt
> was moving.
> "What are you doing?" she asked. Flustered, I managed to reply: "My
> hip's sore and I'm rubbing it."
> "Well, rub it gently. Don't be so vigorous about it."
> Her voice was sleepy.[12]

There is nothing unclear about what is taking place here. It is not
entirely clear, however, whether Dazai intends the passage partly as
indicative of childhood anxiety or wholly as comedy. Inquiring of
Dazai's basic intentions in "Remembrances" one encounters the
same problem. Was Dazai revealing himself, at least his childhood
and adolescent self? Or was he creating an image of himself for purposes of comedy?

Dazai tends to describe his childhood as a period of contentment
and happiness. Yet, despite his use of first-person narration, the portrait seems to be of some self distinct from the author of "Remembrances." As he sketches the figure of his childhood self command-
ing the affection of a grandmother, aunt, and older sisters, Dazai
seems an amused, distant observer of some mildly unbelievable
idyll.

This idyllic world of the child does not endure for very long. First
the maid Take leaves in order to marry; next Dazai's aunt departs
with one of her married daughters. Eventually, when an older sister
dies, a second marries, and two others go off to school, Dazai begins
to look for friends among his schoolmates and his brothers. Several
memorable scenes show the young Dazai taking considerable delight
in his new companions. There are conversations about puppy love
with his younger brother and weekend picnics with school chums at
the ocean. One especially vivid scene shows an older brother bringing a bag of insects to augment a collection Dazai is making as a
school assignment.

Ultimately, however, the author nullifies the import of these
passages by claiming that he is incapable of genuine friendship. At
certain critical moments Dazai breaks free from the public demands
of camaraderie to go off and brood alone. In one notable instance his
classmates call for a strike in order to protest an unjust beating of

Dazai on the part of a certain teacher. The embarrassed Dazai begs them to let the matter drop, but they respond by calling him cowardly and selfish. Thereupon the boy flees to the refuge of a bathhouse.

> A few basho leaves which had survived the autumn winds in the corner of the garden cast a green shadow on the bath water. I sat on the edge of the tub, hardly aware I was alive, drifting into reverie.
> It was my habit to dispel embarrassing memories by muttering to myself "well . . . well." I remembered how I had scurried hither and thither sputtering: "It's nothing, it's nothing." And I repeated to myself, "well . . . well" as I scooped and spilled water, scooped and spilled water.[13]

Dazai explicitly admits in another passage an incapacity for creating strong friendships, an incapacity which he attributes to pride. Instead of honestly revealing himself to others, Dazai invariably seeks to present a fashioned image of himself.

> I was aware of the skinny girl next door, but whenever we passed on the street I looked away as if to make fun of her. One autumn night a fire broke out and I went outside to watch. Flames leapt from the rear of the neighborhood temple against the dark looming background of a cedar grove; birds flitted about like countless falling leaves.
> I knew the girl was watching me as she stood in her white pajamas by the gate of her house, but I kept my gaze on the fire. I figured the side of my face turned toward her would look magnificent in the red glow of the flames.
> Thanks to this habit of tampering, I was unable to deepen my relations with others, with my classmates or this girl.[14]

Anxious as to how he appears to others, Dazai feels a steady constraint in his personal relations. He imagines himself winning the affections of the pretty family maid Miyo; but when he finally contrives one morning to be alone with her in the grape arbor, he bungles his opportunity by faking a rude masculinity that rightly strikes the girl as absurd. Despite his obvious failure Dazai proudly tells himself: "I can relax now that she's mine." The revelation at the end of "Remembrances" that Miyo has been seduced by a household servant and sent away in disgrace does not seem to disturb Dazai. Gazing upon a photo of his aunt and Miyo, he merely takes note of how closely they resemble each other.

Perhaps the act of writing about himself and Miyo was, for Dazai, more significant than any experience he might have shared with her. Throughout "Remembrances" Dazai refers to his propensity for

dramatizing and acting. Sometimes he gathers his friends to act out a
script he has written; at other moments, when he kisses the lips
carved in the desk, for example, he acts out in private his own morbid fantasies. One can reasonably ask, I believe, whether "Remembrances" is not itself a similar kind of act. The following quotation,
already quoted in part, represents the most telling passage in
"Remembrances" on Dazai's purposes in writing, and seems to
foreclose the possibility of confession as a function of the writing.
The words suggest a sense of emptiness and futility in Dazai at the
need to play a multitude of social roles and imply a resolution to shift
the activity of role-playing to a realm that is often thought to be
make-believe, that is, to literature.

One morning, when I was a third-year student in middle-school, I stopped
on my way to class and leaned against the round, lacquer-stained railing of a
bridge. A river about as wide as the Sumida flowed underneath, and, for
several moments, I forgot myself more fully than I ever had before. Usually I
would strike some pose or other in response to a feeling that someone was
watching behind me. Every time I made a move, that someone would stare
at his palms, scratch behind his ear, and mumble at my side. With him
around, I could never act spontaneously.

Recovering from this hypnotic state, I trembled in my loneliness and
pondered again the end to which I had come. I continued across the bridge,
recalling various things, falling again into reverie. At length I let out a sigh
and wondered whether I would become great.

About that time I began to feel anxieties. Satisfied with nothing, ever
struggling in vain. There were ten or twenty masks affixed to my face and I
could no longer discern which was the sorrowing mask, let alone its degree
of sorrow. I finally hit upon a wretched escape: writing. A number of con-
federates joined in this endeavor, and we all seemed to gaze upon the
trepidation we could not understand. Over and over I prayed in secret that I
might become a writer.[15]

IV "*Metamorphosis*"

"Metamorphosis," the title chosen by Thomas J. Harper for his
English translation of the tale, is based on "The Dream Carp" by the
eighteenth-century novelist Ueda Akinari. In Akinari's story a priest
living by Lake Biwa spends his leisure time painting pictures of carp.
Entranced by the carp, the priest dreams that he is transformed into
one of them. He swims gracefully about the lake for a time until he is
hooked by a fisherman. Just as he is about to be sliced into pieces of
sashimi, the priest awakes — only to be told that the events of his
dream have actually occurred. Donald Keene aptly describes the

conclusion as one which leaves the "reader to wonder where to draw
the line between fantasy and reality."[16]

Similarly, in Dazai's "Metamorphosis," a person transformed into
a carp momentarily finds a free and happy existence swimming in
the water. Suwa, the adolescent daughter of a charcoal maker, tends
a small concession selling lemonade and candies to tourists who
come to view a nearby waterfall. Accustomed to her wild environment, Suwa is able to clamber upon the slippery rocks that enclose
the falls and to swim in the treacherous waters below. She is con-
trasted in this respect with a botany student described in retrospect
at one point in the narrative. This student, looking for rare plant
specimens, had fallen from the rocks and drowned.

Carefree at the outset, Suwa becomes melancholy as the tale unfolds. Her father often leaves her to carry his charcoal to town, and
he returns late and reeking of liquor. When Suwa, out of curiosity,
asks what his purpose in life is, her father replies that he is ignorant
of such matters.

One cold night, when her father does not return, Suwa walks in a
partial trance to the waterfall and leaps into the pool. Like the priest
in Akinari's tale, she turns into a carp and swims freely about.
Presently she pauses, as if taking thought, then makes straight for a
whirlpool where her body is swirled around and dragged down "like
a dead leaf."

In "Metamorphosis" Dazai shows that he can readily imitate the
manner of a traditional Japanese fairy tale. In the opening paragraph
of the story, a landmark of red soil in a range of hills is identified as
the spot where Minamoto Yoshitsune's boat struck as it sailed across
the shallow sea that once covered the area. The sentences, typical of
accounts of local legend and lore in Japan, are so matter-of-fact and
casual that skepticism seems irreverent. Dazai's description of Suwa
calling to the tourists at the top of her lungs only to be drowned out
by the waterfall evokes the pathos common to the treatment of
children in Japanese folk literature, and the author's subplot detailing the fate of the brothers Saburo and Hachiro, separated from each
other when Hachiro is turned into a giant snake, implants in the
reader a premonition fulfilled in the tragedy of Suwa.

Conceivably this mastery of traditional methods inhibited Dazai
from reworking the tale into a style more his own. A reader familiar
with Dazai's other works from this period will suspect the hand of his
author on certain occasions in "Metamorphosis," in the surprisingly
mature questions of Suwa, for example, or in the dramatic "second
suicide" of the final scene.[17]

To a degree such occasions in "Metamorphosis" seem almost like intrusions in contrast to the anonymous manner that predominates in the tale. In this respect "Metamorphosis" stands in sharp contrast to Dazai's later efforts in the genre, where his personal tone permeates the retelling of traditional tales.

Given Dazai's repeated attempts at suicide one is prompted to probe for intimations of suicide in "Metamorphosis." Keene's assertion that the carp's descent into the whirlpool represents a "second suicide" must be considered, as well as the suggestion that the seemingly deliberate self-destruction by the carp bespeaks the dangers Dazai sensed in any venture into the realm of the literary imagination. It must be added, however, that "Metamorphosis" provides scant textual justification for comments of this kind. The reader understands neither Suwa nor the carp. He is simply aware of an intangible pressure moving the girl toward suicide.

V *"Monkey Island"*

The first of several Dazai stories concerning monkeys, this moral fable is narrated in the first person by a monkey newly arrived on an unidentified island. The tale is brief, well-knit, and extremely provocative. In the monkey Dazai hit upon a perfect vehicle for rendering his ironic view of reality.

The narrator begins his account by referring to a voyage he has just made across the sea. Inspecting the barren, rocky coast where he has arrived, he eventually discovers an inviting tree, which he proceeds to climb. Although the narrator does not speak of his own identity, the reader already suspects he is a monkey — an impression soon confirmed when a monkey claiming ownership of the tree suddenly appears on the scene.

Despite their initial hostility the two monkeys presently become friends. Thereupon the narrator monkey begins hearing about his new environment. His companion reveals that the *other* monkeys, who inhabit the hilltops, come from an entirely different region. The narrator monkey also learns that shelter and food on the island are provided and that the oddly dressed creatures who pass by regularly serve as a diverting spectacle for the monkeys.

Presently the narrator monkey discovers that his friend has not been entirely candid in his explanations. When two young boys beyond a stone wall gesture toward the two monkeys, the narrator demands of his companion an explanation of their behavior. As his companion grumbles that boys always act that way, the narrator suddenly realizes that the boys are poking fun at the monkeys, that indeed the monkeys serve as a spectacle for these human creatures. The narrator decides to flee the island, in spite of its comforts, and tries to persuade his friend to escape with him. The friend at first proves reluctant, but eventually gives in. The final paragraph of the tale reports in official-sounding prose the escape of two "Japanese monkeys" from a London zoo in mid-June, 1896.

"Monkey Island" demonstrates Dazai's ability to entice a reader to speculate while concealing the final meaning of a fable. In the opening paragraphs the author coyly suggests the nature of the island and its inhabitants before making the facts clear. The narrator calls himself "I" and makes observations and comments exactly as men do; yet the *scale* of the rocks and the island is described by the "I" in terms that suggest an observer much smaller than a man.

In "Monkey Island" Dazai constructed a narrative more integrated than most of his other early works, but he stopped short of writing a full allegory. Within a loosely allegorical frame the actors of "Monkey Island" assume varying symbolic values. Once the story ends these actors are free to continue a half life within the mind of a reader confronting the final puzzle of "Monkey Island."

Is the island simply a thinly disguised version of modern society, whose members enjoy a degree of security and comfort but only enough freedom to make playful gestures and sounds? On which side of the stone wall does the "spectacle" actually take place? Conceivably, a spectacle exists on both sides, with pride alone giving the illusion to beings on either side that they are watching (and not exhibiting) laughable behavior. Finally, if one finds such conditions

Part of the satisfaction in reading "Monkey Island" comes from seeing one's suspicions confirmed. But the finest pleasures of the tale are less tangible. The reader's curiosity is aroused on a number of points and then left unsatisfied. But Dazai works this effect in a manner that leaves the reader to muse instead of feeling cheated. On the simplest level, the question of whether the island represents Japan or England remains moot. The two monkeys seem to have been raised in Japan and to have come across the sea to another island. Their escape at the end of the story from a London zoo would answer the question of the identity of this second island for a literal-minded reader. Yet, the other monkeys on the island are described in ways which conceivably suggest Japanese behavior. And the narrator monkey once remarks that one of the trees growing on the island seems very like an oak common to the Kiso region of central Japan.

of society unendurable and elects to escape, where does flight take him? Further, are questions of this type too conventional an approach to a writer like Dazai? Perhaps, as he claimed in "Remembrances," you escape by writing. The only response to society is to compose a beguiling tale like "Monkey Island."

VI *"Monkey-Face Lad"*

A solemn reader making his way chronologically through Dazai's better-known works could get as far as "Monkey-Face Lad" with merely a suspicion that this author is given to an occasional antic or absurdity. But, having read "Monkey-Face Lad," even such a reader could not overlook Dazai's willingness to turn an entire story into a puzzle or joke. The main character of "Monkey-Face Lad," an anonymous writer, takes up a goodly portion of the narrative detailing his plans for a novel. After literally writing out the first section of his novel within Dazai's "Monkey-Face Lad," the "novelist, after pondering awhile with his eyes on the manuscript, wrote in the title 'Monkey-Face Lad.' He saw in these words the most appropriate tombstone imaginable."

Dazai describes this novelist early in the story in familiar terms. He is a university student married four or five years already to a woman of low status and dependent for his support upon an allowance from his home. At present his main worry is a threat that the allowance will be cancelled, leaving him and his wife to fend for themselves. Though officially a student, he merely makes a pretence of attending classes, for he knows his chances of graduating are almost nil. Already immersed in his writing, he has decided on a career as a novelist.

In the midst of pondering his career and his novel-in-progress, the protagonist enters a used book store looking for inspiration. The plot hatched in his strange imagination is divided into three scenes. In the first of these an aspiring writer receives a postcard from a young woman who tries to console him for the failure of his first novel. The following two scenes each involve a letter. The protagonist receives a letter after being jailed as a revolutionary, and finally he catches sight of a letter of no particular significance written by his wife. In glancing at this third letter the novelist realizes that his wife draws a particular ideogram in a style identical to that used in the two earlier missives. Obviously, the reader is meant to draw the conclusion, never explicitly put by Dazai, that the wife wrote the postcard and the earlier letter also.

VII *"He Is Not What He Was"*

Dazai recalled the English expression "he is not what he was" from a childhood lesson in English grammar. For the title of the present story Dazai fashioned a Japanese expression with the same meaning as the English and, in the body of the story, he actually quotes the English. A title such as "He Is Never the Same" would sum up the theme of the work more precisely, but it seems best to allow Dazai to title his own work.

A landlord, who narrates the story in the first person, has rented his house to a strange tenant named Kenoshita Aogi. Addressing an undefined listener, the landlord reveals that Aogi, the third tenant to rent the house, first represented himself as a calligraphy teacher of the "Unfettered Genius School." Relying on the landlord's goodwill, Aogi receives permission to settle in the house before depositing the rent and the key money commonly required in Japan.

For the most part, the tale comprises a series of visits by the landlord to Aogi, visits initially undertaken in a futile attempt to collect the rent. Aogi at first puts off the landlord with plausible excuses and promises. Eventually it dawns on the landlord that Aogi is never going to pay. In the course of his visits the landlord discovers additional reasons to doubt Aogi's reliability. His tenant often speaks in riddles and makes a number of odd claims for himself, that he served as the model for the hero of Mori Ogai's novel, *The Youth*, to cite one example. Three women live with Aogi in less than a year, the first of whom flatly tells the landlord that his tenant is not to be trusted.

By the time he realizes that Aogi is hardly a worthwhile risk, the landlord has begun to experience a mixture of fear and sympathy toward his tenant that impedes him from acting on a businesslike basis. Once, striking a match to light his cigarette, the landlord sees Aogi's face as that "of a demon." Again, he conceives the possibility that Aogi's eccentric manner is simply the young man's way of affording visitors to his house some entertainment.

However, after tolerating Aogi for almost a year, the landlord seems to arrive at the conclusion that he has become overgenerous in his judgment of the tenant. Aogi's changes of mood and behavior are not the manipulations of a fine comic spirit; they are merely slight "changes in coloration" that transpire from day to day in accord with the weather. Ending his narration, the landlord turns to the listener whose presence has been merely implied throughout the work:

Look at Aogi, strolling along in his striped cloak in that vacant lot with a paper kite flying above. Now, what's got into you, laughing without a letup? . . . There's a resemblance? Stop it! All right, I'll put the question to you. Between *that* fellow gazing up at the sky, shrugging his shoulders, letting his head droop, and tearing leaves off the trees as he goes by — between *him* and *me* standing right here — is there even one point of difference?[18]

This sudden prominence of the landlord in the final sentence is hardly consonant with the principal concerns of "He Is Not What He Was." For almost the entire story the landlord is a secondary figure serving primarily to convey to the reader an impression of the strange Aogi. Of necessity something of the landlord's character, his timidity and goodwill, for example, becomes evident. Further, when he speculates that Aogi's odd behavior springs from his conviction that his landlord expects him to behave that way, it seems possible that the landlord functions as a catalyst as well as narrator of events.

Nevertheless, his manner of narration draws only slight attention to the landlord as a personality. The reader sees him exactly as the landlord sees himself, as one bemused by a mysterious tenant. Only in the opening paragraph, where the narrator draws his listener's attention to Aogi by a circuitous geographical description, and in the closing words already quoted is there any suggestion that the landlord possesses the peculiar élan that one associates with important characters in Dazai's fiction.

With the narrator in the background, the interest through most of the tale lies in the motivations of Aogi's strange behavior. From the very beginning any reader will suspect that Aogi's main purpose in his meetings with the landlord is to avoid paying the rent. If this is his aim, several factors favor his success in the endeavor. The landlord appears to be an older, tradition-minded Japanese, reluctant to speak out in any offensive way and almost completely unwilling to discuss money matters. Initially, Aogi, with the help of his first "wife," manipulates the landlord by admitting the very worst about himself. His boldness puts the landlord in an uncomfortable position. Admitting that he lied in representing himself as a calligraphy teacher, Aogi explains that the ruse was necessary in order to find a landlord willing to rent him a place. Rendered speechless by Aogi's boldness, the landlord has no choice but to ignore the problem of the rent.

During the latter half of "He Is Not What He Was," the landlord conceives other explanations for Aogi's behavior. Perhaps Aogi plays the eccentric deliberately as a means of entertaining his guests. Nothing in the story tends to confirm this particular intuition of the landlord. However, it must be noted that Aogi does resemble Dazai in various ways, and that Dazai was formulating during this period his notion of "art as the service of entertaining."

The landlord conceives a second, somewhat counter explanation for Aogi's behavior just when he begins to grow weary of his tenant. A weak personality with no center of his own, Aogi simply responds to the mood and demeanor of his companion of the moment. This particular interpretation receives indirect support from the suggestion at the end of the story that the landlord is indeed a twin of the weird Aogi.

These ambiguities and blurrings tend to make "He Is Not What He Was" the incomprehensible piece that Dazai perhaps intended. It seems unlikely that the riddles outlined above were meant to be answered by the story. After all, the fun of reading "He Is Not What He Was" rests largely in one's uncertainty as to why Aogi treats the landlord in such bewildering ways; the fun of pondering the story lies in one's uncertainty as to whether the landlord has hit upon the truth in his final remark — a remark directed at the listener-reader of "He Is Not What He Was."

VIII *"Romanesque"*

Along with "Metamorphosis," "Romanesque" demonstrates Dazai's early interest in folklore and legend. For narratives of this kind Dazai employs a relatively plain, direct style in keeping with the simplicity of his subject matter. His individuality as author tends to reveal itself principally in the peculiar turns of event which the stories take on occasion.

"Romanesque" consists of three independent tales tied together in the coda of the third piece. Each of these tales has as its title the name and epithet of the principal character. The first, entitled "Magician Taro," describes the wondrous career of a weird, gifted youngster. Taro begins to display his uniqueness even in infancy. Rather than move instinctively to suckle at his mother's breast, Taro opens his mouth wide and waits for the breast to come to him. Straying from home one day before he has learned to speak, Taro is discovered mumbling incoherent words on a hill overlooking the village. Upon reflection his father, the village headman, interprets Taro's words as a prediction that the land will prosper. After the village prospers a number of years, a flood visits devastation on the area. Whereupon Taro, now in his early teens, sets out on his own to successfully petition the local daimyo for the aid that will enable the people to survive and prosper again.

Taro is never drawn to any of the usual pursuits of childhood and adolescence. Ignoring the other children in the neighborhood, he spends his time indoors contriving riddles. Once he asks his father what can enter water without getting wet. (The answer, which escapes his father, turns out to be "shadows.") This interest leads eventually to a sustained investigation of the occult. A young man now, Taro masters the ancient art of transformation and spends his time in the family library turning alternately into a mouse, an eagle, and a snake. Having fallen in love, he studies how to transform himself into a handsome man. Much to his chagrin he turns himself into a handsome man according to the ideals of the Tempyo Period (mid-eighth century) when the book was written.

Dazai emphasizes this image of Taro as disconsolate in the concluding lines of the tale: "They say that Taro's secret involved folding his arms, leaning against a pillar or fence, and chanting over and over in a trance: dull, dull, dull, dull, dull. . . . Eventually he would escape from himself."[19]

Dazai's second tale in "Romanesque" concerns the exploits of "Jiro Heibei the Wrangler." The son of a sake brewer, Jiro Heibei scorns the family business to such a degree that, whenever he inadvertently drinks some of its sake, he forces himself to cough up every drop. Ignored by the respectable people of the town and laughed to shame by his fellow tipplers after a clumsy attempt at chivalry, Jiro Heibei decides to turn himself into the "complete wrangler."

Dazai traces Jiro's development with precision. Determined to forego the use of weapons, the young man begins training by toughening his fist on such objects as tavern tables and the tobacco tray at his bedside. Next, transferring his practice to a tree stump, he perfects the aim of his punch. Finally, he advances to a moving target, the waterwheels that keep the melted runoff from Mount Fuji flowing through town. After three years of training Jiro Heibei pronounces himself fit and begins looking for an argument.

So muscular and intimidating has he become that no worthy candidate appears to accept his challenge. Named fire chief through the influence of his father, Jiro Heibei almost manages to provoke a fight with the gruff proprietor of a rival sake firm whose house must be hosed down to prevent a fire in a neighboring building from spreading. Eventually the brash fellow finds an opportunity to demonstrate his skill, but it turns out to be disastrous for him. One day he gives his bride one playful tap to the forehead, another to the stomach, and, lo and behold, she falls over dead. Jiro Heibei is condemned to jail, but he commands among his fellow prisoners the respect due a leader.

The third and final tale of "Romanesque" involves a relatively philosophical character, "Saburo the Liar." Early in the work Saburo is placed several times in circumstances that prompt him to tell amusing lies. When a neighbor's barking dog prevents him and his father from sleeping one night, Saburo quiets the animal with a rock.

It struck the dog in the head. One sharp shriek, and the small white body twirled like a top, collapsed, and died. After Saburo closed the shutters and tucked himself into bed, his father inquired in a drowsy voice: "Well, what happened?" Saburo replied without removing the covers from his face: "He stopped howling. He's so sick he'll probably be dead by tomorrow."[20]

Eventually, Saburo becomes a chronic liar and begins putting to practical use his abilities in this regard. The students who pursue Chinese studies under his scholarly father are constantly in need of money, and Saburo obliges them by contriving letters that always succeed in touching the heart and pocketbook of a fond parent. Finally Saburo writes a profitable series of *sharebon*, witty stories based on life in the gay quarters of Tokugawa Japan.

Although Saburo remains irrepressible to the end, he seems, in the final words of the story, to escape his role as a sport and become a spokesman for Dazai. Dazai prepares his reader for this new image of Saburo by sounding a somber note on occasion during the course of the narrative. He describes the beating of the drum at the funeral of Saburo's father in terms that apply equally to much of his own writing: "The mad rhythms drummed by the priest seemed barbaric at first; but, listening with care, one could detect within those rhythms an unbearable impatience and anger, along with a desperate humor that tried to make light of these feelings."[21]

Toward the end of the tale Saburo is regarded as such a liar that even the words of his resolve at the funeral to lead an "honest life" are themselves a lie. When Saburo meets Magician Taro and Jiro Heibei the Wrangler in the final scene and proclaims that "we three are all artists," the reader is quite willing to accept Dazai's claim that this too is a lie. Given the nature of Dazai's preoccupations, perhaps one is justified in entertaining the notion that the author is not simply dismissing Saburo, but soberly stating that *art itself is a lie.*

IX   *The Flower of Buffoonery*

The Flower of Buffoonery, published in 1935, was initially intended to form part of *Final Years.* Based on Dazai's double suicide attempt at Kamakura and the succeeding days spent in recuperation at a nearby hospital, *The Flower of Buffoonery* is intimately connected with the despair that motivated the entire writing project and suggested the title *Final Years.* Eventually, Dazai removed *The Flower of Buffoonery* from *Final Years* and incorporated it as one member of a trilogy entitled *Wanderings of Falsehood.*

Most of *The Flower of Buffoonery* takes place in the hospital room of Oba Yozo, who is recovering from shock and a few bruises sustained in his unsuccessful suicide attempt. Hida and Kosuge, two of Yozo's friends, arrive for a visit. Constrained at first in their approach to Yozo, Hida and Kosuge presently find themselves laughing and frolicking with their friend just as in the days before the suicide attempt. Much of the laughter seems hollow and the antics are always downright silly.

On occasion a sober mood comes over the room. Once Yozo's older brother, representing the family, arrives to lecture the young man on his responsibilities and to forestall any possible scandal. In addition, the hospital director, who observes Yozo's recuperation, often casts a pall over the room with his dignified presence.

The nurse, Mano, who keeps constant watch on Yozo, is a sobering presence in the long run. Early in the story Mano tends to join with the playful spirit of the three friends. She laughs when they laugh and even springs to their defense when the head nurse criticizes them for their raucous behavior. As the story unfolds, however, Mano becomes serious. One night she tells Yozo how a childhood accident inflicted the scar above her eye. She goes on to explain that she was teased by other children and, in reaction, vowed to accomplish something of significance. She admits that, in retrospect, such a vow was foolishly unrealistic.

In the final scene of *The Flower of Buffoonery,* Yozo and Mano go for an early morning walk in the hills overlooking the sea. Evidently it is their last time together, for Yozo is scheduled to be released from the hospital the same day. After describing the disappointment of Mano and Yozo at finding Mount Fuji hidden by clouds, Dazai concludes his story: "Yozo looked all the way down to the sea. Enoshima seemed very small at the bottom of the hill. The ocean moved sluggishly in the heavy morning fog. Then . . . no . . . That's all there is to it."[22]

Although *The Flower of Buffoonery* concentrates mainly on Yozo's recuperation, the narrative turns retrospectively on occasion to the process leading up to the suicide attempt. Yozo had no specific reason for wishing to destroy himself. The woman with whom he attempted suicide was not the lover of a traditional *joshi*,[23] but a chance acquaintance for whom he felt no special affection. At one point in the narrative, Yozo, recalling his leap into the sea, muses how every personal problem disappears with death. "Debts, school, home, regrets, masterpieces, shame, Marxism. Your friends too, and the woods and flowers. When I realized that nothing would matter any more, I laughed out loud. . . . What a relief."[24] In brief, everything conspires toward Yozo's suicide.

Attempting to rehabilitate their friend, Hida and Kosuge try to put Yozo in a state of unbroken giddiness wherein he will not have the leisure to brood. Early in the story, with the nurse Mano assisting, this effort appears to be succeeding. Later, however, Hida and Kosuge have a falling-out with Mano. Learning that the head nurse has reprimanded Mano for the noise emanating from Yozo's room, Hida and Kosuge act outraged and urge a counterattack. Mano takes their words seriously and marches toward the corridor to put their urging into effect, whereupon the two men suddenly turn sober and hasten to hold her back. No scene illustrates so clearly as this that Hida and Kosuge do not mean what they say; they talk simply to sustain a mood. For this point on, instead of allying herself with the comic spirit of Yozo's friends, Mano begins talking to Yozo in serious terms. She speaks of her unfortunate childhood first. Then she relates a haunting episode from her nursing experience: a crab from a nearby beach crawled into the hospital room where she was keeping an all-night vigil over the corpse of a suicide. In the final scene of *The Flower of Buffoonery*, Mano accompanies Yozo to the cliff overlooking Enoshima. Dazai does not reveal Yozo's reaction as he gazes down at the slowly moving sea. But one can readily discern the options posed for Yozo in this confrontation with the possibility of suicide: to ignore his problems by joining in the pranks of Hida and Kosuge, or to face (and hopefully transcend) the appeal of death.

The narrative provides nothing additional on the dilemma faced by Oba Yozo. It must be said, however, that Yozo is not the only person in *The Flower of Buffoonery* confronting the choice between a carefree, meaningless style of life and a brooding, questing way that holds promise of meaning.

The Flower of Buffoonery begins in the following manner:

"Beyond here, a place of sorrows." My friends all gaze mournfully at me from a distance. Speak to me, friends, laugh at me. They simply turn away. Question me, friends. I'll tell everything. I shoved Sono under the waves with this hand. In demonic pride I wished death for her and survival for myself. Shall I go on? My friends merely gaze mournfully at me.

Oba Yozo sat up in bed and looked out at the sea. The offing was dim in the rain.

Waking from a dream, I read over these lines. I felt like disappearing into shame and loathing. Well, the exaggeration's reached a limit; now, to get on with it, just who is this Oba Yozo?[25]

Even for Dazai, this is an extreme manipulation of the "I." Yozo begins the narration as a first-person observer undergoing a reverie. But, in a moment he is interrupted by the author, who breaks into the narration as a second "I." The opening passage sets a pattern for the whole of *The Flower of Buffoonery*. On the one hand there is Oba Yozo, the protagonist struggling with a crucial personal problem; and, on the other hand, there is Dazai Osamu struggling to tell Yozo's story. Doubtless a biographical-minded critic would regard these two figures as identical.

In a sense Yozo and Dazai are identical. The manner in which Dazai intrudes to comment within the narrative, however, tends on occasion to emphasize his function as author separate from the work. For example, pretending to an exasperation at his inability to properly develop the plot, Dazai calls *The Flower of Buffoonery* "senile" and himself a "third-rate author." In another passage he conceives of his novel becoming a classic, then labels himself crazy for entertaining such a thought.

Dazai begins another of his interruptions purporting to explain the purpose of the intrusions.

I'll tell everything. In truth, it was just a scheme of mine to thrust this fellow called "I" in between scenes and have him recite things he should have left unsaid. Without letting the reader notice what was afoot, I strove to impart a special nuance to the work with this "I." I congratulated myself on a grand style hitherto lacking in Japanese letters. But I failed. Why, even this confession of failure I've included in my plans. I wanted it in a little later, if possible. And, I think I arranged to say *that* from the beginning too. Ah . . . don't listen to me. Don't listen to a thing I say.[26]

In a later passage Dazai again declares that involving himself in the work was a mistake.

I've said much that should not have been said. Moreover, I've a feeling that I've overlooked more important matters. This may sound priggish — but, if I pick up this work later, I'll feel wretched. I'll tremble in self-disgust even before I finish a page. I'll close it surely, I don't even have the heart to read what I've done now. Ah, a writer can't afford to reveal himself. That's his downfall.[27]

Needless to say, his reader can hardly take Dazai literally. He had already shown that he could destroy manuscripts that did not satisfy him, and if Dazai had in fact despised *The Flower of Buffoonery*, the manuscript would have ended up in the backyard fire.

Dazai feigns an uncertainty as to how to relate his story until the very end. Recall the final line, which follows immediately Yozo's contemplation of the sea below: "Then . . . no . . . that's all there is to it." Dazai, it would appear, is not suggesting that Yozo has transcended his fears. The author, to put it baldly, is unable himself to continue narrating. For he *is* Yozo, not simply in the sense that he is writing an autobiography of past experience, but, more significantly, in the sense that he as well as Yozo does not know what step to take next.

X *A Style and Manner Characteristic of Dazai*

Dazai's development as a writer underwent a considerable shift when he moved from his native Tsugaru to Tokyo in 1930. While a student in middle and higher school, Dazai was serving his apprenticeship. Evidently, during this early period, he conceived of a novel or story in a manner similar to that of the Japanese proletarian writer: a straightforward narrative embodying the relatively definite and unitary views of the author. The difficulties Dazai seems to have felt in formulating a plot during the apprenticeship period were avoided to a degree in the works treated in the present chapter. He began writing a few relatively overt autobiographical pieces, along with anecdotal and fabliaulike tales exemplifying various notions about society. Such works freed Dazai to insert authorial comment and to manipulate the steps of his plot with great boldness.

Already by this period Dazai had developed the knack of *fixing* a character in a scene with a few brief words, rather than rendering character with an accumulation of detail. The reader remembers a few telling details — the behavior of Ryuji's mother on the train for Tokyo or the sudden plunge of the carp in "Metamorphosis." As Donald Keene has perceptively written, "One never has the impression that Dazai has carefully filled notebooks with observations so that he will be able to provide local color when needed. Instead the reader senses that each scene has been distilled through Dazai's poetic imagination into its essential ingredients."[28] For precisely this reason a reader familiar with Dazai can readily accept the patchwork construction of such a work as "Leaves."

These sudden perceptions in Dazai's works often seem to relate to the author's life. When Dazai does not compose straight autobiography, he is often writing disguised autobiography. He may be speaking merely of a monkey or a boy; but the reader who goes through his work chronologically senses in a certain gesture or remark that Dazai is present in the boy or the monkey. Once initiated into the Dazai manner, a reader can easily begin to take the works as clever exercises in covert autobiography.

Yet, Dazai is not pinned down so readily. For one thing, he is exceedingly elusive at the game of hide-and-seek. Perhaps his style is best described by the image he creates showing one of those moments of odd behavior in his youth — the time when, mimicking the walk of a geisha, he would glance sideways at shop windows to catch his own reflection. Like Dazai in this scene, the reader, too, must be quick and see through the disguise.

Clearly, Dazai wants his readers to see *him*. He is neither wearing a mask, in the manner of a Mishima, nor entering into a persona, in the manner of a Yeats or a Pound. He is not much concerned with creating a social self distinct from the person, nor with extending the range of his experience through imagining characters beyond his experience. Dazai's mask is like the Halloween kind; he wears it in fun, to give his friends a momentary thrill. And there is seldom any doubt as to who is actually wearing the mask.

It is tempting, then, to see in Dazai an entrepreneur of comedy. But the presence of such a work as *The Flower of Buffoonery* gives one pause. Dazai sees the pathos and potential self-destruction in the kind of comedy he practiced both in life and in writing. Any full account of his career must, above all, come to grips with the tragicomedy of Dazai Osamu.

CHAPTER 3

The Prewar Years (1935-1941)

I   The Biography

ONE evening in March, 1935, Dazai went again to Kamakura and attempted suicide. No doubt mindful of his earlier failure in the same locale, this time he went alone and chose a method which fright or a sudden change of heart would not easily thwart. But the following day he showed up in Tokyo — much to the relief of his worried friends — with only a vicious rope burn circling his neck.

Within ten days of his return from Kamakura, Dazai suffered a powerful attack of appendicitis that brought him closer to death than any of his suicide attempts. Two days after the operation, he coughed up so much blood that even his doctor gave up hope. But Dazai rallied to such an extent that he was soon transferred to a second hospital to be treated for contagious tuberculosis. He remained under treatment until the middle of the summer, when he left for the town of Funabashi in Chiba Prefecture to complete his recovery. Dazai testified later to the enjoyable life he led at Funabashi pattering about the town with the help of a cane and tending a plum orchard in his backyard. His brother sent a monthly sum of money sufficient to cover living expenses for both Dazai and Hatsuyo.

At the same time, it was, as Dazai would later admit, one of the most fateful periods of his life — a period which could not but strengthen his belief that he was a man destined for condemnation. After his appendicitis operation the doctors had authorized the use of drugs to alleviate Dazai's pain. The changing of the bandages each evening was especially trying, and the patient was liberally drugged to help him endure the pain. Dazai found the drugs pleasant as well as helpful. He confessed in "Eight Views of Tokyo" that his continued use of drugs once he had moved to Funabashi was more to cure his loneliness and anxiety than to deaden any physical pain. Unfortunately, he was able to find a doctor willing to indulge his complaints of insomnia by writing a prescription.

Dazai remained in Funabashi until October, 1936. During this time he began to come to public attention as a writer. His first volume of stories, *Final Years*, was published as a collection and he was nominated several times for the newly instituted Akutagawa Prize. Yet his private life was in decline. The allowance his brother sent proved insufficient to cover Dazai's increasing need for drugs. So he began to appear at the offices of various publishers in Tokyo, asking for an advance on a story or begging for a commission to write a novel. At the urging of friends, Dazai agreed to commit himself for treatment, but left the hospital before anything could be accomplished.

Finally Dazai's friends, Ibuse Masuji in particular, decided to take matters into their own hands. Ibuse put the request to Dazai as persuasively as possible: "You will be doing me the greatest possible favor if you enter the hospital for care."[1] Dazai could not refuse the mentor who had been so solicitous for his success.[2] So he let himself be taken from his pleasant Funabashi home to the Musashino Hospital. Only when he found himself locked alone in a cell did he wake up to the fact that his friends had put him in a mental institution.

It was indeed a traumatic experience for Dazai. His fear that he belonged to some subhuman, "twilight" zone had been publicly validated. Indeed, the few friends Dazai thought he could trust had conspired with the institutions of society to mark him thus. When he was released after a month's confinement, Dazai characteristically began a work based on his experience with the English title "Human Lost." Shortly before his death after the war, he still felt moved to write of this event. His greatest work in the opinion of most Japanese critics purports to be the notebook of a "madman" confined for a time in an asylum.

Dazai's trust in his fellow human beings received a second great shock the spring of the following year. A friend confided to Dazai that Hatsuyo had carried on an affair with an acquaintance of the author's while he was in the hospital. Confronted by Dazai in a scene reminiscent of an earlier occasion,[3] Hatsuyo not only confessed her transgression but asked Dazai for permission to marry her lover. When the man in question fled shortly after, Dazai seized the opportunity to invite Hatsuyo to commit suicide. Together they took a train from Ueno Station to Minakami, a famous hot spring resort in

Gumma Prefecture. There Dazai administered sleeping pills to both
Hatsuyo and himself and also rigged up a complicated piece of gear
by which to hang himself from a cliff. Both survived the ordeal,
returned to Tokyo, and separated. Hatsuyo went back to Aomori
while Dazai resumed a bachelor's life in Tokyo. Predictably, a story
entitled "Forsaking the Old Woman" appeared two years later
describing an unsuccessful double suicide attempt at the Minakami
hot spring resort.

For almost a year and a half Dazai merely loafed, keeping himself
alive on the small allowance which arrived on schedule each month
from Kanagi. He lived alone for a while in Tokyo in a small, four-
mat room, drinking cheap sake, and going outside in the evening to
lean against a nearby gate and whistle songs to himself. Later he
visited Ibuse Masuji at Miyakejima for a week. Returning to Tokyo,
he passed his time drinking and playing cards with such friends as
Dan Kazuo and Yamagishi Gaishi. One chore alone remained to an-
noy him. He had to chase his friends away and clean his room once a
month to make a satisfactory impression on the agent his brother
sent around to check on him. During the entire period from April,
1937, to September, 1938, with the exception of a single, slight story
entitled "The Votive Lantern," Dazai wrote nothing that was
published.

Late in the summer of 1935, while recovering from his appendicitis operation at Funabashi, Dazai wrote a work with the German title
"Das Gemeine," or "The Vulgar." Written for the library periodical *Literature: Spring and Autumn*, "Das Gemeine" was published
in October as part of a series of commissioned works. In all, four
works were commissioned, one by each of the four writers — including Dazai — who had lost in the final competition for the first Akutagawa Literary Prize;[4] awarded to Ishikawa Tatsuzo. Sato Haruo has
described how anxious Dazai was to capture the Akutagawa award.
Dazai's chagrin at losing by a close margin was such that he showed
no admiration for Ishikawa's winning story and was at best patroniz-
ing about the works contributed by the other losing candidates.

In September, 1936, one month before Dazai was tricked into letting himself be taken to a mental hospital, there appeared in the
journal *Young Grass* a slim piece entitled "Cheers." "Cheers"
begins with Dazai's declaration — a paradoxical one — of his
freedom as an artist. "I write only what I do not want to write. I
create only those forms which seem difficult to express. I deny
utterly the ethic of the bourgeois strolling about town with his

department store bag."[5] Then Dazai proceeds to describe his activities as an aspiring writer. He tells of the trials encountered in publishing the first numbers of the literary magazine *Cell Literature*, particularly the vast amount of monotonous editorial work. By his own reckoning, Dazai did most of the work.

Despite the self-pity, Dazai felt he was participating to some extent in a group project. At the outset of the article he refers enthusiastically to his associates — Ibuse Masuji, Hayashi Fusao, Kuno Toyohiko, Funabashi Seiichi, Funito Ikuyoshi, Inoue Kojiro, and others. Admittedly, "Cheers" is not, in literary terms, a significant work in the Dazai canon. Yet, critics turn it to good use by citing it as proof that Dazai felt great trust in certain people — Ibuse Masuji, most notably — who were about to betray him. As Okuno Tateo has remarked, "In 'Cheers,' written shortly before his hospitalization, Dazai showed an innocent, overflowing trust in his mentors and friends."[6]

The thoughts which plagued Dazai as he lay trapped for a month in the asylum were recorded in the form of a poetic diary published with the English title "Human Lost." In it he claimed that his friend's betrayal and his internment determined the course of his future life. Dazai, it should be remembered, had just experienced his first taste of public acclaim with the publication of *Final Years*. Several accounts of the party given at the Seiyoken Restaurant in Ueno Park by his publisher and friends to celebrate the occasion agree in portraying Dazai as overjoyed to the point of ecstasy. Also he was beginning to receive commissions from periodicals for articles and was himself venturing into publishing with *Cell Literature*. Dazai, then, had gained a measure of recognition from his elders and peers. Further, he no doubt saw an opportunity to free himself from the debts his drug addiction was causing — and, perhaps, even from financial dependence on his older brother who was still sending him a monthly allowance.

"Human Lost" is a curious, flat work. After one has finished reading it, very little — other than the title — remains in the memory. There are strictures against Hatsuyo. They are not specific, however, and the reader does not know whether to attribute them to the anger Dazai felt when he learned of her infidelity — an interpretation requiring that the passages in question not refer to Dazai's state of mind during his hospitalization — or to his suspicion that she had cooperated with Ibuse in getting him into the hospital. This vagueness is present from the very beginning of the work:

Showa 11:   October 13.   Nothing.
            October 14.   Nothing.
            October 15.   Profound feeling.
            October 16.   Nothing.
            October 17.   Nothing.
            October 18.   Broke my fan in two while
                          opening it.[7]

Dazai was probably not in a creative mood anyway. Abandoning hope for success as a writer, he makes one of his earliest references to Christ, a figure who would become abruptly prominent in certain later works. "I avoided, with an enthusiastic 'amen,' the demanding academic fencing of the older writers exemplified by Satomi and Shimazaki. I pursued knowledge only to attain the humility of Christ."[8]

With the publication of "Human Lost" in April, 1937, Dazai, with the exception of the slight story "The Votive Lantern," fell into a silence that continued for a full year and a half. This silence and the lighter tone of the works following it show more eloquently than "Human Lost" that Dazai's betrayal and hospitalization had indeed wrought some basic change.

In "A Yearbook of Agonies," written shortly after the end of World War II, Dazai Osamu acknowledged that his outlook on life had undergone fundamental changes several times. Yet, he insisted, no one particular event or thought process could account for these changes. Like the weather, they merely occurred.

"Early in the summer of my thirtieth year, I felt for the first time a serious desire to become a writer."[9] The reader of Dazai might object to his author's short memory on this point. But Dazai probably felt that, for no reason in particular, he had been resurrected from his malaise of a year and a half. Perhaps he felt that the new creative urge originated from yet untouched springs. As he expressed it, he was writing now to live, not, as in the instance of *Final Years*, to die.

Dazai published two stories, "Forsaking the Old Woman"[10] and "The Fulfillment of a Vow," in September, 1938. With the commission from his work he reclaimed some of his clothes from the pawnshops and began looking for a new residence. With the help of Ibuse Masuji he took lodgings at an inn near Kofu and began plotting a long novel.

Dazai appeared to be regaining his zest for life; but his acquaintances, familiar with his sudden shifts of mood, were still on edge.

Kita Hojiro, and Nakabatake Keikichi, representing Dazai's family, approached Ibuse Masuji and timidly inquired whether Dazai did not have a girl friend. The family in Aomori felt that Dazai would be more secure if he were properly married, yet — because of Dazai's unsavory reputation — was unwilling itself to secure a bride in the locale.[11] At the behest of the two men, Ibuse Masuji undertook the task.

On January 8, 1939, Dazai, in the presence of Ibuse, Kita, Nakabatake, and relatives of the bride, was married in Tokyo to Miss Ishihara Michiko, an instructress at the Tsuru Girls' Higher School. Neither Miss Ishihara, the first candidate Ibuse uncovered, nor her mother was very impressed with Dazai initially. Michiko, having read descriptions of Dazai's character and behavior in Sato Haruo's *The Akutagawa Prize*, fretted about her prospective husband's unreliability; her mother, after her meeting with Dazai, confided to Ibuse that Dazai was like a child.

It was Dazai's persistence, along with a radical change in his character, that apparently won their consent to the match. Dazai remained at his inn near Kofu, partly to work on a new novel to be called *Bird of Fire*, partly to await the outcome of his proposal. Ibuse Masuji, for one, was duly impressed with Dazai's new seriousness. Returning from Tokyo late in the fall for the engagement ceremony to be held in Kofu, Ibuse arrived at the inn when Dazai happened to be away:

> With the first glance I was struck with amazement at how "prettily" Dazai had arranged his desk. One could see how keenly he had appreciated the autumn colors at this mountain inn. I remembered his room at Ogikubo. Truly a different person was living in the room upon which I now gazed.[12]

It appears that Dazai, for whatever reasons, was anxious to marry Ishihara Michiko. Characteristically, he set his mind on the match on the spur of the moment — precisely at the moment he saw her for the first time after taking notice of a photo of Mount Fuji in the living room of her home in Kofu. This juxtaposition of Michiko and Mount Fuji has some significance. Dazai, from his vantage point at the inn near Kofu, was greatly impressed by the sight of Fuji's lovely grace. Recalling his impressions, he published in 1939 a sketch whose title reflects Hiroshige, "One Hundred Views of Mount Fuji."

Dazai's sincerity about the proposed marriage can hardly be called into question. With no assistance from his family — ordinarily a fatal blow in cases of a proposed arranged marriage — he convinced the doubtful girl and her mother that he was a good risk. Trusting to his newly discovered creative energies, writing now — as he expressed it — "to live rather than to die," Dazai himself looked confidently to the future. He had had, we may assume, no more than the three small cups of sake usually drunk by the bridegroom when he declared to the gathering at the wedding ceremony: "I can't thank you enough. Keep watch on the future. I'm not the kind of person to forget my obligations. I'll watch my health, of course, but I won't spare myself. You'll see how far I develop this talent of mine."[13]

Dazai's resolution to pursue a stable life was so firm that many critics and commentators sarcastically call this his "bourgeois period." Dazai himself testified in "The Fifteen Year Era" that this was the happiest, most stable period of his life.

At first, he lived in Kofu, the city where his wife had taught in the girls' higher school. Located in a plain west of Tokyo on the Koshu Highway, Kofu, like the capital, is subject to humid summers. Dazai, who grew up almost on the northern tip of Honshu, persevered till August. The move to Mitaka Village — now Mitaka City in Tokyo — could hardly have brought any relief from the weather. But, Dazai pointed out to his wife, he would be conveniently close to the publishers.

He was doubtless anxious to be close to them, for he was writing with a feverishness reminiscent of his *Final Years* period. The number of works is impressive: "One Hundred Views of Mount Fuji," "Girl Student," "A Lazy Game of Cards," "Cherry Leaves and the Devil's Flute," "The Word of a Young Tree," "Flower Candle," "Eighty-eight Nights," "Beautiful Maiden," "A Talk about Dog-keeping." However, with the exception of "One Hundred Views of Mount Fuji," Japanese critics on the whole have not been very impressed with the quality of these stories.

It will be well to give a few glimpses of what these first several years of Dazai's married life — before the arrival of children — were like. Michiko served at times as her husband's secretary, taking down, for example, the whole text of "Golden Landscape" as Dazai dictated it. Again, during the trying summer at Kofu, Michiko contracted prickly heat. Thereupon Dazai accompanied her each morning through the dewy fields to a neighboring hot spring reputed to be a good cure for prickly heat, an experience which provided a basis for the short story "Beautiful Maiden." With the move to Mitaka nothing occurred to upset the even keel of the marriage. Some of

Dazai's old cronies, as well as the neighbor and critic Kamei Kat-suichiro and some younger students attracted by Dazai's growing reputation, came to visit. Dazai frequently went out for a drink and had his daily quota of sake at home each evening. Nothing untoward happened; no one wrote even a colorful description of Dazai gruffly ordering his wife in the Tsugaru dialect (as he had done to Hatsuyo) to serve the sake and the dried cuttlefish.

Dazai had indeed joined his old enemy, the bourgeois. He was earnest in his work; even when he used inn stationery to do some writing while on a trip, he wrote at the top of each sheet the characters "*bunpitsugyo*," that is, "literary profession." The fact that he began to take trips — something which in his earlier "pover-ty" he had reviled as a waste of time and money — was itself in-dicative. He traveled to Gumma Prefecture, to Niigata, and even as far as Sado Island in the Sea of Japan. At Niigata he even delivered a lecture to a high school audience. Several times he traveled to the Izu Peninsula, joining his wife for the return trip on one of these oc-casions for what they termed their "honeymoon."

During 1939 and 1940 Dazai for the most part remained at his Mitaka home writing at a good pace. The quantity does not match his Kofu output; but Japanese critics tend to regard the later works, especially "Sea Gull," "The Indictment," and "Run Melos," more highly. One piece, "A Spring Burglar," stands out more for its in-dication of things to come than for its literary merit.

Published in 1940 in the January issue of *Literature Japan* with the subtitle "My Poem from Jail," "A Spring Burglar" represents Dazai's "longing for freedom from the prison of his bourgeois ex-istence."[14] If his wife read the work she must have recalled the early doubts inspired by Sato Haruo's remarks. Perhaps the demon in Dazai had only lain dormant for several years without being put per-manently to rest.

You slip in, snatch up the cash, and take off. Is that all there is to it? There's nothing romantic about this world of mine.

I'm the only degenerate around here. Yet I too now make my way through the world industriously following the bourgeois code. Disgusting!

Even if I must do it alone, I want to leap once more into that romantic hell of ambition and striving. Is that impossible? Is that forbidden?[15]

In "Eight Views of Tokyo," the main source of information of his life in Tokyo until the time of his marriage to Ishihara Michiko, Dazai mentioned that his brother had dropped him from the family register shortly after his suicide attempt with Hatsuyo at the Minakami Hot Spring. At the same time, the family was meeting other misfortunes. A sister and a nephew of Dazai's died, and his brother was indicted on a charge of election fraud.

Rather than gloat over the misfortunes of his family, Dazai achieved in writing about them a degree of objectivity thitherto often lacking. In "Eight Views of Tokyo," for example, he dwelt with sympathy on his relations with his family and his earlier experience with the sick brother studying sculpture in Tokyo. A short piece entitled "Older Brothers," probably written in late 1939, describes essentially the same areas of Dazai's life with objective restraint.

With Hatsuyo's return to Aomori, Dazai began to lose interest in his family. With a few exceptions they ceased to provide material for his fiction. For his story situations he relied instead on his own thoughts and experiences and on other literary works that called to mind his own predicaments.

The optimism that followed Dazai's resolution to reform his life appears most conspicuously in "One Hundred Views of Mount Fuji." Written for the most part during the early months of marriage at Kofu, "One Hundred Views of Mount Fuji" was published in the February and March numbers of the periodical *Literary Style* in 1939. The work, a straightforward autobiography, describes Dazai's experiences as he lived in an inn near Kofu awaiting the outcome of his marriage proposal. Perhaps the very success of the venture prompted Dazai to look back indulgently upon his sojourn at the inn.

Dazai spent some of the happiest days of his life during the first few months of marriage with his bride in Kofu. By the time he moved to Mitaka in September, 1938, his happiness had subsided into routine contentment. Even in picturing himself as a settled husband, though, Dazai could not avoid a note of uneasiness:

> The fools say that I have become a plebian. The setting sun seems very large each evening from Musashino. It falls tremulously as though sinking into a boiling cauldron.
> Sitting with crossed legs in a three-mat room to watch the spectacle during my meager supper, I confide to my wife: "I'll never get rich or cut a figure in the world living like this. But, somehow or other, I want to preserve what we have.[16]

In "Sea Gull," a work published in January, 1940, Dazai showed himself giving way to discontent. His depression expressed itself in familiar ways; yet there was at least one entirely new reason for it. The war with China had grown to such proportions that men of Dazai's age were rapidly being inducted. In "Sea Gull," Dazai tried to justify himself as a patriot. Unable to pass the physical examination for induction, Dazai wrote in despair: "I can do nothing." Even the one talent in which he felt some confidence failed him. Referring to accusations (whether actual or only in his mind Dazai does not say) that he is guilty of laxity in refusing to write about the war, Dazai protests: "Until I grope about and finally feel the thing, I cannot write a word about it."

Despite his efforts, Dazai was steadily falling victim to his old neurosis. The "Human Lost" theme recurs throughout the work: "I have lost my humanity." The old fear that fate had dealt harshly with him also appears: "I was born with an inferior character." The resolution to reform and the zest with which he undertook his marriage had given way to despair. "I float about — now this way now that — wheresoever the waves take me."

Like "Sea Gull," "A Spring Burglar," published in January, 1940, is a miscellany of Dazai's thoughts and moods. Here Dazai does not appear so lackadaisical. He realized that he could indeed exercise an option: to continue his current uneventful life as a model husband, or to throw himself into his former dissipation. Dazai found the bourgeoisie too restricting, declaring at one point (quoted earlier in this chapter) that he wished "to leap once more into that romantic hell of ambition and striving."

His attitude at certain moments, though, took a more complicated form. He wished to make the best of two worlds, plunging into his "romantic hell," but preserving appearances at the same time.

More than anything else I wish to speak with authority. If others regard what I say as eccentric, I'd rather be silent. In that event my passions will remain hidden behind a genial mask.

Our society takes as its gospel only the statements of those routine creatures who lead respectable lives. To consciously plan one's behavior so no one can point the finger — to cleverly abide by the mores of society — then you can show them. You can write, just as you please, a murder novel or an even more frightening novel or essay.

Ogai[17] was clever at this. He carried off the affair perfectly with a completely innocent air. I want to try it. I'd be content to do half as well. I shall not be satisfied with mediocrity; I shall instead take utter revenge upon it.[18]

II *"Das Gemeine"*

In choosing the title "Das Gemeine," Dazai seems to have had in mind more than the meaning of the word itself. The final three syllables would be pronounced "ma-i-ne" in Japanese and thus mark the negative imperative form of the verb in the author's Tsugaru dialect. However, the story does not appear to be predicted on a relation between the terms "vulgar" and "must not."

Indeed, "Das Gemeine" bristles with problems for the reader seeking to analyze it. Dazai seems even less bound by literary convention than was usual for him. A character named Sano Jiro is the first-person narrator until nearly the end of the story, when he is struck by a train and killed. Sano confesses to an overwhelming love for a mystery woman at the beginning of the story, but his beloved turns out to be a prostitute who is shown to the reader only as she sits at the window of a brothel attracting customers. In addition to specific oddities of this kind, the general plot, consisting of conversations almost unrelated to each other, seems uncommonly bizarre.

In the beginning our narrator Sano Jiro meets a strange man named Baba at a stand serving sweet sake in Tokyo's Ueno Park. Baba claims to be a music student who has attended the conservatory eight years without taking a single examination. He expresses a number of unconventional opinions with which Sano finds himself in agreement: that it is wholly degrading for one person to try to measure the skill and ability of another by an examination, for example, or that the carrying case is more important than the violin inside.

After Sano and Baba become friends, the latter broaches the idea of starting a literary magazine to be called *The Pirate*. Seeking help for the magazine, Baba solicits the financial assistance of his friend Satake and the literary talents of an aspiring novelist named Dazai Osamu. A meeting of the four men to discuss the venture quickly breaks up, thanks to certain fatuous remarks by Dazai.

There follows a conversation between Baba and Sano Jiro, during which the latter begins to doubt the integrity of Baba. Taking leave of his companion, Sano Jiro seems to lapse into an hypnotic state, which Dazai describes in the following manner: "Run, train. Run, Sano Jiro. Run, train. Run, Sano Jiro. He chants over and over in a reckless rhythm. Ah, this is my creation. The sole poem I've composed. What a mess! Because I'm stupid. Because I'm stupid. Light. Explosion. Star. Leaf. Signal. Wind. Ah!"[19]

In a brief dialogue that concludes the work, Satake explains to

Baba that he has earned two hundred yen in hopes of spending a convivial evening with Sano Jiro. Baba takes Satake's money and, after giving half to the serving-girl of the sweet sake stand for a new kimono and sash, invites Satake for an evening of fun.

As this summary suggests, the diverse occurrences in "Das Gemeine" are seldom related by the operations of logical causality. Only a few events in the work seem even distantly related to one another in narrative terms. Sano Jiro believes at first in the sincerity of Baba, despite the preposterous claims the latter makes for himself. (Baba insists, for example, that *he* composed the lovely music for Doi Bansui's "Moon over the Ruined Castle," using the name of the man universally taken to be the composer, Take Rentaro.) Evidently, the shock given to this faith by Baba's tentative confession that he is an imposter puts Sano Jiro into the dazed state during which he wanders into the path of a train.

There are some relations between "Das Gemeine" and other works of literature. Dazai found the full name of his protagonist, Sano Jiro Saemon, in the Kabuki play *Kagotsurube Sato no Eizame*, whose hero, a self-made man of means disfigured by smallpox, falls in love with a Yoshiwara geisha only to kill her after she spurns his love. Other works by Dazai himself are thematically related to "Das Gemeine." In the postwar story, "Villon's Wife," for instance, one finds the same casual attitude toward tragic events that Baba shows toward the death of Sano Jiro.

In the main, though, "Das Gemeine" seems a deliberate attempt by Dazai to create a feeling of disorientation toward life. It is occasionally said that Dazai fashioned a style for "Das Gemeine" under the influence of Dadaism and Surrealism which had begun to make their way into Japanese literature in the late 1920's. The passage already quoted describing the final moments of Sano Jiro is cited as an example of this abrupt, staccato style, as well as the opening words of the story: "In love. It was absolutely the first time."

Precisely because the story is disjointed, "Das Gemeine" presents certain of Dazai's characteristic methods of style in high relief. Baba's plan of launching a literary periodical serves Dazai principally as a means of bringing together a strange group of characters, two of which are described in the following manner:

Satake's smooth, delicate face gave the impression of a milk-white, highly polished No mask. The pupils of the eyes seemed like tinted glass, with no definite focus. The cold, ivory miniature of the thin, knifelike nose, the eyebrows long and thin like willow-leaves, the thin lips strawberry red. In comparison to this striking face, the arms and legs were surprisingly meager, He was barely five feet tall, with the small, shriveled palms of a lizard. He remained standing and began speaking to me in the soft, dead voice of an old man.[20]

The second figure described is at least as bizarre as Satake.

A hack writer from the word go. He's got a big, sallow face that glistens with oil. And his nose — I've read about a nose like that in Regnier. A supremely precarious nose, with deep wrinkles on the side that just keep it from collapsing into a "dumpling nose." Exactly! Regnier's got it exactly. The eyebrows are wide and black, and almost bushy enough to cover his tiny, darting eyes. The eyelid seems stubbornly narrow, with two deeply carved wrinkles — it's just incredible! From the back, his hair hangs in a line about a thick neck, he looks like a dunce. And, let's see, I noticed three red pimple scars on his neck — just below the jaw.[21]

After continuing in this vein, the speaker of these words declares he has been lying and attempts a second description:

The guy's got a face smooth as an egg — no eyes, no mouth, no eyebrows. At least, what eyebrows are there seem painted on, and the eyes and nose glued on. And the *art* he makes of showing you this nonchalance. Christ! The first time I looked at him, I felt like a tongue of gluten paste was wiping across my face.[22]

Thus does the author allow one of his characters to describe the oddest figure of all in "Das Gemeine," writer Dazai Osamu.

III   *"Foresaking the Old Woman"*

Dazai's title derives from a legend associated with a mountain in Nagano Prefecture. According to the legend, a man, at the urging of his wife, once took his aged mother up the mountain and left her to die. However, watching the bright moon after his return home, the man came to feel bitter regret over his cruelty. The following day he went again to the mountain and carried his mother back to safety.

Dazai's "Forsaking the Old Woman" deals with a married couple who travel from Tokyo to the Minakami Hot Spring area to commit double suicide. Kazue, the wife, has decided to commit suicide in reparation for committing adultery; her husband, Kishichi, wishes to die with her because he believes he drove Kazue to be unfaithful.

The opening scenes of "Foresaking the Old Woman" show the couple in Tokyo making preparations for the trip to Minakami. They pawn some of their belongings in order to purchase sleeping pills and train tickets. They also go to a movie and enjoy a final meal at a *sushi* shop.

Departing on the evening train, they reach Minakami about dawn and immediately go to a small inn where they are known. After relaxing a day at the inn, they set off as though they intend to return to Tokyo. Heading down the mountain slope toward Minakami, they peer into the woods in hopes of discovering an inviting place to carry out the double suicide.

An appropriate place is found. Kishichi doles out a few pills to Kazue, then swallows a large number himself, washing them down with spring water and instructing Kazue to do likewise. Leaving Kazue to herself, Kishichi makes his way to the edge of a cliff. Aware that even the large number of pills he has swallowed will only knock him unconscious, Kishichi ties one end of his sash to a tree and knots the other end about his neck.

Later, Kishichi wakes up with a chilled feeling and finds himself resting in a pool of cold spring water. A brief search brings him to Kazue, still alive at the bottom of the cliff. The couple remain in the woods to regain their strength and, after they emerge, Kazue returns to the inn, Kishichi to Tokyo. Their double suicide attempt a failure, the couple agree to a separation.

In "Eight Views of Tokyo," an autobiographical sketch of his early years in Tokyo, Dazai claimed that "Forsaking the Old Woman" was based directly on the double suicide attempt at Minakami Hot Spring by Hatsuyo and himself. One must take Dazai's word for the actuality of certain events in the story; however, the truth of such occurrences as Hatsuyo's infidelity and the separation of Hatsuyo and Dazai is beyond question.

Like many other works by Dazai, "Forsaking the Old Woman" raises the question of whether the author was seriously examining a tragic problem or utilizing a situation for comic purposes. For people about to commit suicide, Kazue and Kishichi are incredibly blithe. Their only fear is that someone will sense their intention and put a stop to their plan. They become tense when buying the sleeping pills and when the mistress at the inn runs after them with a parting gift as they depart in the direction of Minakami. With admirable consistency, neither Kazue nor Kishichi is relieved in the least at coming through the ordeal with impunity.

This nonchalance toward the prospect of death manifests itself on a number of occasions. Kishichi and Kazue arrive at the decision to commit suicide in the midst of a half-jesting conversation with each other. Just before the train leaves Tokyo, Kazue runs to buy a bag of chestnuts for the mistress at the inn near Minakami.

In addition to the light moments, there are scenes bordering on farce. One of these has already been mentioned: the awakening of Kishichi from the suicide attempt, his rump cold and wet in the spring water. Another possibly farcical scene occurs on the train to Minakami. During a long monologue to which Kazue pays scant attention, Kishichi offers a justification for leading a degenerate life. In a series of platitudes that some critics regard as crucial for understanding Dazai, Kishichi claims that "Christ's mercy shines in proportion to Judas's sin" and that a holy light shines in proportion to the evil wrought by destructive beings. Kishichi seems in dead ernest, and, when Kazue ignores his words, he stands up and staggers toward the toilet. "He entered and slammed the door. Then, after a moment's hesitation, he placed his palms together. It was a figure praying, and *not* a pose."

Scenes of this nature, which occur in other works, raise a fundamental issue concerning Dazai's art. Dazai says that Kishichi is not posing, and many of his readers will no doubt agree that Kishichi is not posing. Nonetheless, the fact remains that Dazai *chose* to describe Kishichi in a posture that appears melodramatic. Readers aware of the autobiographical dimension of "Forsaking the Old Woman" might argue that Dazai was merely describing what happened on the way to Minakami. But this perfectly sensible response simply moves the doubt from Dazai's literary work square into his life. When Japanese critics accuse Dazai of "striking a pose," they seem to be claiming that he deliberately contrived his life to enable himself to write autobiographical pieces consonant with his particular stylistic skills. The idiosyncratic nature of Dazai's life and certain of his works lends credence to this explanation. Yet, if one is tempted to accept such an extreme claim, he ought to probe for the motives that drove Dazai to put his life to such an unconventional use.

IV *"One Hundred Views of Mount Fuji"*

"One Hundred Views of Mount Fuji" describes the author's sojourn during the autumn of 1938 at an inn near the Misaka Pass, reputedly one of the three finest places from which to view the famous mountain. Although Dazai asserted in another work from the same period, with the English title "I Can Speak," that he found the social isolation and cold weather of Misaka Pass unbearable, he describes his stay at the inn in "One Hundred Views of Mount Fuji" as a relatively enjoyable experience.

Having redeemed some clothes from a pawnshop, Dazai sets out for Misaka in a jaunty mood, leaving behind in Tokyo the bitter memories surrounding the abortive suicide attempt at Minakami. At first it seems that Dazai is merely seeking a change of mood and the chance to see his old mentor, Ibuse Masuji, currently residing at the inn. After enjoying one another's company for several days, Ibuse and Dazai descend to the nearby city of Kofu for a visit Ibuse has evidently been arranging. It is the first meeting, or *o-miai*, between Dazai and Ishihara Michiko, the woman who is to become his second wife.

Dazai returns alone to the inn at Misaka to continue working on the novel *Bird of Fire* and to await the outcome of the marriage negotiation. Life at the inn is enlivened by occasional visits from tourists or curiosity-seekers, but Dazai's main interest seems to be the prospective marriage. Although the family in Kanagi offers no assistance whatever, Ishihara Michiko and her mother are sufficiently impressed by Dazai to discount the family. Michiko's mother once tells Dazai that "affection" and "enthusiasm for one's line of work" are the most important considerations. Dazai, for his part, seems quite taken with Michiko. Catching a glimpse of her for the first time as his gaze moves from a photo of Mount Fuji in the Ishihara parlor, Dazai tells himself: "It's decided. . . . I want to marry her. Thank you, Mount Fuji."

Did the whim actually strike Dazai in this manner? Or did he doctor his account to show what a lighthearted fellow he could be in making a normally serious decision? The reader of "One Hundred Views of Mount Fuji" experiences a similar uncertainty when Dazai returns to the inn after learning that Michiko and her mother are favorably disposed toward him. Dazai asks one of the maids to give him a massage to relieve the tension of his visit to Kofu. But so ineffective is the girl that Dazai eventually orders her to pummel him with logs. Perhaps Dazai is merely relating facts. But one again suspects that his main purpose is to use facts for their amusement value.

Though characteristic of Dazai, this ambiguity of intention is not common in "One Hundred Views of Mount Fuji." In a number of scenes Dazai appears as the practiced raconteur, deftly sketching whatever strikes his fancy. He describes himself and Ibuse climbing to an observation point above Misaka for a view of Mount Fuji only to discover that fog has obscured the mountain. Ibuse sits down on a rock, puffing on his cigarette and manifesting chagrin with a fart. Then the old proprietress of a nearby teahouse restores the men to their earlier good spirits by hauling forth a huge photo of Mount Fuji, which she props at the edge of the lookout in order to demonstrate what one can see on a clear day.

Mount Fuji serves as a backdrop for other amusing scenes. Toward the end of Dazai's stay at the inn, a young woman in wedding dress arrives at the pass with two old men in formal dress. Observing the bride yawn at the sight of Mount Fuji, Dazai concludes that this must be her second or third marriage. Another incident involves two giggling schoolgirls who ask Dazai to take a photo of them with Mount Fuji in the background. After listening with mock seriousness to the girls' instructions, Dazai maneuvers the camera to photograph the mountain unmarred by the presence of the girls.

Dazai's most striking encounter with Mount Fuji takes the unusual form of a mystical reverie. Having spent an evening drinking with several worshipful students, Dazai decides to pass the rest of the night in an inn at the foot of the mountain. Unable to sleep, he puts on a padded kimono and goes out.

The moon fearfully bright, Mount Fuji superb. Pale and transparent in the light, I felt as though a fox were bewitching me. Fuji blue and melting. A sense of phosphorous burning. Devil's fire. Fox fire. Firefly. Tall grass. Arrowroot leaf. I walked straight down the road unaware of my legs. A pair of *geta* echoed — *karan, karon, karan, karon* — like a living creature other than myself. I turned slowly about. There was Fuji, a blue flame floating in the sky. I let out a sigh. Patriot of the Revolution. Kurama Tengu. Thus I thought myself. With some affectation I folded my arms and walked on. I felt like a really superb chap.

I had dropped my purse. Too heavy anyway, with twenty silver coins. Probably the purse had slipped from my pocket. I was perfectly calm. No problem to walk as far as Misaka without money. So I walked on. Then I realized that retracing my steps would bring me to the purse. I strolled back, arms folded. Fuji. Moon-filled night. Patriot of the Revolution, dropping his purse. Surely an intriguing romance. The purse glistened in the middle of the road. Inevitably. I picked up my money, returned to the inn, and slept.[23]

V *"The Indictment"*

Ishihara Michiko has revealed that Dazai dictated to her the entire text of "The Indictment" in one sitting without pausing to search for words. Although Dazai is known to have dictated other works to Michiko, none seems to have poured from him so readily as "The Indictment." Indeed, this tour de force was doubtless made possible by the narrative method of "The Indictment," a rapid monologue by Judas Iscariot explaining before the high priest his motives for betraying Christ.

In essence, Judas's monologue is a resentful tirade against Christ. Scornful of supernatural claims, Judas regards Christ's references to the Heavenly Kingdom and Son of God as pure nonsense. Drawn to Christ physically, Judas pays homage to the beauty of his lord and vents his strongest resentments against those for whom Christ expresses affection.

Like his biblical counterpart, Dazai's Judas serves as treasurer for Christ and the apostles. Proud of his skillful management of the purse, Judas feels indignant at Christ's negative attitude toward money. How, Judas wonders, could a person be so lacking in discernment as to expect him to feed a large crowd with just five loaves and two fishes on hand? Why drive from the temple such an influential group as the money-changers?

Regarding himself as superior to the other apostles, Judas finds Christ's jaundiced view of himself hard to bear. For Judas, the other apostles are avaricious bores hungry for the wealth the promised kingdom will bring. Peter is the supreme dunce, especially at the Last Supper when, in order to secure the greatest possible benefit, he demands that Christ wash his entire body rather than his feet alone. How galling for Judas that Christ favors a man like Peter over himself.

During his long tirade Judas leaps so rapidly from one thought to the next that he often loses track of what he has said. So effectively does he give the impression of blurting out his thoughts that one is completely surprised to hear him confess at the end that he has fabricated the entire explanation. In fact, Judas tells the high priest, he has betrayed Christ for the thirty pieces of silver. Treasurer to the last, Judas affirms that the "way of the world is money, pure and simple."

So firm are these final words that one is tempted to regard them as the definitive interpretation of the entire monologue. A more thorough reading of the story, however, would give equal weight to the earlier explanations Judas offers of his betrayal. Given what appears to be the spontaneity of his speech, it is hard to believe that Judas has deliberately spun out a commentary that conceals his real motive, only to nullify his effort in the end with a frank confession. More important, accepting the truth of Judas's final confession turns Dazai's story into a meaningless exercise in the rhetoric of pleading.

Several Japanese critics, including Okuno Tateo, accept Judas's confession as the truth. Normally, this view sees Judas as foul and evil in contrast to the purity and goodness of Christ. Okuno, for example, castigates Judas as "possessive to the point of blindness and unaware of the great love and sorrow of Christ."

Citing Christ as a value-object in "The Indictment," however, raises several problems. First, it is impossible to determine from "The Indictment" just how Dazai himself judged Christ. Who can say that his judgment did not coincide with the judgment of Judas? Second, the most trenchant criticisms of Christ in Judas's monologue have sufficient point and precision to withstand a dismissal in generalized, spiritual terms. One cannot read "The Indictment" without realizing on occasion that Judas has a good case against Christ. Judas recalls for the reader of Dazai the protagonist of "Landlord for a Generation," a narrator so prejudiced he does not feel the need to doctor the facts as he understands them. Like this earlier narrator, Judas assures his credibility by the contradictory nature of his speech; unlike the landlord, however, Judas does not expose himself as a fool. At first glance, one aspect of the first-person narration of "The Indictment" seems unusual for Dazai. Judas indicates, by his repeated use of the word *danna*, or "master," that the high priest is listening to his account. Some might argue, on the basis of this awareness, that Dazai was examining the way in which Judas would try to justify himself in a public forum. Nevertheless, the more plausible argument is that Dazai has not changed one whit from his earlier method of allowing his first-person narrators to blurt out their feelings directly. The rhythms of Judas's speech suggest a man driven to the breaking point, a man desperate to salve his wounded pride by angrily abusing the one who has rejected him. To attribute craft, guile, or even presence of mind to Dazai's Judas seems utterly unwarranted.

VI   *"Run Melos"*

Maintaining a steady pace, Dazai published what many Japanese regard as one of his greatest short stories, "Run Melos." This judgment is surprising in view of the general tendency in Japan to value the author's more somber works, whose dark mood is relieved only on occasion by flashes of mordant, sarcastic humor. Dazai's best lengthy works in a lighter vein, *A Collection of Fairy Tales* and *A Retelling of the Tales from the Provinces*, are among those least known to the Japanese reading public. "Run Melos," though, is possibly the brightest, most optimistic work in the entire Dazai canon.

In "Run Melos" Dazai set out to write a tale exemplifying the highest kind of fidelity. Seemingly unable to use his own experience in pursuing such a theme and chronically plagued (so he claimed) by a weak imagination for the creation of plot, Dazai chose as his source a work by Schiller entitled "Die Burgschaft" (The Hostage).

Dazai's version is essentially a retelling of the Schiller work, with certain additions characteristic of Dazai. In Dazai's version the young shepherd Melos, accompanied by a lifelong friend, goes to Syracuse to make some purchases in preparation for the wedding of his younger sister. Informed that the local king is a tyrant, the valiant Melos enters the palace to save the city from this scourge. Apprehended and brought before the king, Melos unabashedly proclaims his rebellion, whereupon the king sentences him to death by crucifixion. Recalling that he must return home for his sister's wedding, Melos offers his friend as a hostage, promising to return for his punishment in three days.

After the wedding Melos braves such obstacles as a flooding river and a host of mountain bandits while hurrying back to Syracuse to keep his promise. Exhausted, he once falls down by the roadside exclaiming: "Virtue, fidelity, love! When you think about it, they're nonsense. Kill your opponent and protect yourself. Isn't that the way of the world?" Awakened by the sound of running water, he changes his mind: "I gave my word. That's the only consideration. Run, Melos!"

Predictably, he arrives to find his friend hoisted aloft, but still alive. He immediately tells the friend of his momentary loss of faith. Then he asks the friend to strike him hard on both cheeks so he, Melos, can feel free to embrace him before going to his death. After doing as instructed, the friend asks for the same treatment from Melos. The friend, it turns out, had himself momentarily lost faith in Melos's word that he would return to redeem the hostage. The king is so impressed by the friendship and loyalty of Melos and his friend that he not only reprieves Melos but asks both of the friends to take him into their friendship.

Stylistically, "Run Melos" is pure Dazai. Probably such passages as the description of Melos frantically running toward Syracuse account in large part for the tale's reputation in Japan: "Pushing aside and leaping over the people on the road, Melos ran like the wind. Cutting across a field he raced directly through a drinking party, upending all guests. Then he kicked aside a dog and leapt into a river, fleeing ten times as fast as the slowly sinking sun."[24]

The student of Dazai also recognizes his author's hand in the additions Dazai makes to Schiller's original tale. In Schiller there is no doubting by either party of his friend's fidelity and hence no confessions of such doubt. Again, Dazai has his Melos preach to his sister that, once a person begins distrusting others, he will soon begin to tell lies. Finally, in an episode which catches the reader by surprise, the king declares that Melos and his friend could never understand the loneliness of a king. It was characteristic of Dazai to have the villain in a story make a direct, moving appeal for sympathy.

VII   "Beggar-Student"

Eventually the student of Dazai comes to realize that he must qualify every claim he makes concerning the autobiographical character of a work by his author. "Beggar-Student," which relates the strange adventure of a self-deprecating novelist, seems overtly autobiographical. The novelist is Dazai Osamu, resident of Mitaka; he is thirty-two years old, he has hairy shins. All the references fit, except one. After revealing that Dazai Osamu is a pseudonym, the protagonist gives his real name as Kimura Takeo.

The author begins "Beggar-Student" by skillfully evoking the disgust with which a writer mails an inferior manuscript to his publisher. Having deposited such a manuscript in the mailbox by Mitaka Station, protagonist Dazai Osamu feels too depressed to return home. Hoping to lift his spirits, he heads toward Inogashira Park for a walk.

Following the Tamagawa Watercourse, Dazai catches sight of a naked man being swept downstream, shouting that he is freezing to death. Dazai runs toward the stream, knowing he cannot swim well enough to effect a rescue. But, in his present mood, he wouldn't mind dying, so he runs on. Then, in a curious sequence of events, he trips over a tree root but keeps running through tall grass said to be infested with snakes, pulling up short when a voice suddenly berates him, "What a nasty bastard, kicking me in the stomach like that!" The speaker turns out to be the swimmer, now resting stark naked in the grass.

Dazai and his antagonist, a youngster named Saeki Goichiro, fall into a verbal duel. At first, Saeki uses his quick wit and strong intuitive sense to keep Dazai on the defensive. Dazai can only claim that, since he is older than Saeki, his own opinions and judgments should prevail.

Presently Dazai's persistent probing finds a chink in Saeki's armor. In order to attend higher school, Saeki, the "Beggar-Student" of the title, has accepted the patronage of a politician named Hayama. Saeki has agreed to tutor Hayama's daughter, but he has been saddled with additional chores. Saeki confesses to Dazai the most galling of these chores: his pupil plans to make her tutor serve as commentator when she shows her friends the movies she has taken during a recent vacation in Hokkaido.

After offering some fatherly advice on the necessity of enduring unpleasantness in youth, Dazai rashly insists on taking Saeki's place as commentator. The two men then journey to Shibuya to secure from Saeki's friend a student uniform for Dazai. After a series of spats leading to Saeki's admission that the movie has already been shown, the three companions stroll about the Shibuya area of Tokyo in search of a spot to eat and drink. Eventually they get drunk and merry — whereupon Dazai breaks into a song of nostalgia for lost youth. Called to order by a policeman, Dazai hears a second voice calling. Immediately he is awake and aware of familiar surroundings: the Tamagawa Watercourse flowing through Inogashira Park. The student Saeki, impeccably dressed, stands alongside looking down at Dazai. From the moment of the swimming scene, the author has merely dreamed the events of "Beggar-Student."

Obviously, it was necessary to describe the events of "Beggar-Student" as though they were occurring simultaneously with Dazai's account of them. Given the effect of spontaneity characteristic of his style, this was probably no great tour de force for Dazai: simply by avoiding the past and perfect tenses and concocting a title other than "Remembrances," he could without special effort convey the required effect.

Here, it is necessary to examine briefly Dazai's use of a dream as part of his narrative framework. Though a common technique in both classical and modern Japanese literature, the dream is seldom used by Dazai. In "Beggar-Student" the dream is closely tied to one of Dazai's basic themes. In his short commentary on the work, Okuno Tateo calls attention to the difference in quality between dream-life and real-life. Dazai the protagonist is quite lively in the dream, especially in the company of the two students; in the final paragraphs of the story, alone with himself in reality, he is utterly depressed. In the end Dazai recognizes in himself the same dull, thirty-two-year-old novelist who deposited a manuscript in a mailbox at the outset of the narrative.

Even during the dream, however, Dazai reveals certain truths about his real self. During the argument with Saeki, he acknowledges in an aside to the reader that he lacks the social finesse to relate to his fellow man. In earlier works Dazai confessed to a proud self-awareness that prevented him from making the natural, spontaneous gestures that create friendship. In "Beggar-Student" he seems to put the onus for his failure in friendship on a kind of "one-upmanship" often practiced by the Japanese in the give-and-take of conversation.

It is frequently asserted that the Japanese are shy and withdrawn in a social situation. There is a grain of truth to this assertion, especially in cases where the Japanese finds himself in a relation totally new or foreign. Nevertheless, in their daily relations with kin and close friends, many Japanese are self-assertive to a brutal degree.

In his verbal duel with Dazai, Saeki reveals the self-assurance and the unconcern for the feelings of his opponent that almost guarantee him victory. Dazai, on the contrary, lacking the gift of repartee, senses an almost certain defeat. Fortunately, he is able to shift the site of the battle and implement new tactics between his first encounter with Saeki at the Tamagawa Watercourse and the trip to Shibuya. He persuades Saeki to accompany him to the concession booth by the pond in Inogashira Park. Dazai knows from experience that people sitting near the pond look at the water rather than at one another. Under the hypnotic spell of the water and the trees beyond, Dazai finally succeeds in getting the upper hand over his opponent.

VIII   The New Hamlet

Following "Beggar-Student," published serially in the magazine *Young Grass* from July to December, 1940, Dazai's next significant work, published in *Literature: Spring and Autumn* in July, 1941, was a long novel in dramatic form, *The New Hamlet*. Like most of Dazai's adaptations from Western sources, *The New Hamlet* resembles its prototype only on the surface. Inside, as Dazai proudly declared in the preface, much is different, most notably, the "new Hamlet" himself.

One need only read the first act to see why Dazai, with some reason, chose his subject. Without a great deal of juggling, Hamlet and certain of his actions take on a resemblance to Dazai and his experience. Hamlet's very ambiguity, permitting great leeway for specifying certain actions, was a boon to Dazai. There is no need, for instance, to probe the new Hamlet's feelings toward his mother. He is, for Dazai, precisely what Joseph Anderson and Donald Richie have claimed he is for the educated Japanese: "little more than a faithful son avenging his father's death; one who loves his mother not in Olivier's Oedipus-like fashion but merely as every good boy should."[25]

Hamlet is Dazai-like in numerous ways. "Since his infancy," Gertrude declares, "he has been a clever cry-baby." When King Claudius remarks much more concretely than in Shakespeare on Hamlet's height, thinness, and poor facial color, the image is clearly that of Dazai. When Claudius refuses to permit Hamlet to go to Wittenberg for fear he will merely dissipate, one is almost forcibly reminded of Dazai's profligate ways in Tokyo. Again, Hamlet's ancestry is mediocre — inferior perhaps to what Dazai imagined his own to be.

Hamlet himself expresses many of his author's personal beliefs and attitudes. Polonius, charging Hamlet that his speech is all affectation, draws a strong rejoinder: "I always speak precisely what I think." Again, Hamlet sums up his own nature in a passage that Okuno Tateo calls the "most important clue to the understanding of Dazai."

From the earliest times I felt neither malice nor contempt, neither anger nor envy. Imitating others, I made a great display of contempt and malice, but these feelings were hardly genuine. Pity sometimes swept over me in a series of waves and this alone, during my twenty-three years of life, has truly moved me.[26]

Nevertheless, Dazai's attitude toward Hamlet, like his attitude toward himself, is deliberately ironical. Other characters give free rein to their criticisms of Hamlet. To Claudius he is inflexible and hypocritical. To Gertrude he is foppish, reckless, tied to the past, and — of course — a cry-baby. Laertes and Polonius accuse him of affectation, and even Ophelia, pregnant with Hamlet's child, delivers a long tirade at one point summing up just about all these criticisms.

Dazai's Hamlet shares to a degree the irony and self-detachment of his prototype. Still, he is quick at times, as the quoted passage on the "truth" of his own speech suggests, to come to his own defense. More characteristically, he simply tries to outdo the criticisms others direct at him: "I suppose I'm an indulgent drunkard. A disgusting, affected creature. I don't mind. If that's the way things are, it can't be helped." These very remarks, though, set the stage for a series of self-compliments — although backhanded ones — a few lines later in the same speech: "I know my own shortcomings and vices, know them with almost unbearable clarity. I'm no sophist, nor am I a social climber. I'm simply a realist. I'm aware of everything — just as it is."[27]

Readers with some experience of Japanese fiction, classical as well as modern, realize they are expected to accept the self-valuation of main characters much more readily than in reading Western fiction.[28] Dazai wants his readers to accept the "new Hamlet" at face value rather than to ask what sort of neurosis prompts him to make such a declaration.

Presumably, then, Dazai's theme is Hamlet's "honesty." Unfortunately, Hamlet is never faced with a situation where honesty entails any sacrifice. He is, indeed, sufficiently honest not to play along with the deceit of the others. When, for example, Claudius, recognizing that Hamlet hates him, asks him to conceal his hatred for the good of the state, Hamlet ignores the offer and asks leave to attend the university at Wittenberg. Yet, he is never pushed to the limit where, like the original Hamlet, he might be stung into action to remove the corruption in Denmark.

In the end the "new Hamlet" is more a buffoon than a tragic hero. Claudius has admitted that he planned to kill Hamlet's father, but claims the latter died before he could accomplish his purpose. Hamlet pulls out his sword, readies himself to avenge his father on Claudius, then slashes himself superficially across the cheek. Thereupon Horatio reports that Gertrude has committed suicide. The play ends with Hamlet and Claudius in an unseemly spat over which one of them has suffered more.

Two additional points important for Dazai's later development deserve mention. His habit of referring to and quoting the Bible, already evident in "The Indictment," is continued in *The New Hamlet*. Hamlet, arguing against Ophelia's identification of silence and love, quotes Saint Paul on love. That "the thing is recorded in the Bible" seems to him sufficient to quell all dispute.

More significantly, Ophelia, pregnant with Hamlet's child, voices a sentiment that will bulk large in Dazai's postwar work, *The Setting Sun* in particular. Ophelia is singularly unperturbed at the prospect that the new Hamlet might prove to be an unreliable father. In reply to Gertrude's criticism of Hamlet and her unfavorable comparison of Hamlet to Laertes, Ophelia replies that she will be content to raise Hamlet's child alone.

The scene — like others in *The New Hamlet* — strikes the reader with greater impact for having no precedent in Shakespeare's play. But the Dazai scholar need not cast far for the source. Dazai, by the reckoning of Okuno Tateo, began writing *The New Hamlet* at the beginning of February, 1941. The work was published in July of that year, just one month after Dazai became a father for the first time.

IX   *A Period of Crises*

Although he was well on his way to becoming an established writer, Dazai Osamu continued to experiment with great energy during the second half of the 1930's. This experimentation was not, I believe, a duplication of the first apprenticeship period of Dazai's career. Rather, the sudden and marked shifts in the writing during these years must reflect to some degree the drastic transformation in the author's personal life: the shock of being confined to an asylum, the mild palliative of domestic tranquillity, and finally the urge to escape the stifling atmosphere of marriage manifesting itself in a renewed life of dissipation.

The range of Dazai's experimentation reveals itself in the vastly different works of this period. Some, like "Das Gemeine" and "Human Lost," seem eccentric and pointless; others, like "One Hundred Views of Mount Fuji" and "Run Melos," are optimistic and light; finally, works like "The Indictment" contain a message of desperation expressed with great clarity and craft.

Certain writings during this period suggest the intriguing possibility that Dazai could most readily see himself with detachment when he wrote within the constraining influence of traditional Japanese culture. A brief comparison between "Das Gemeine" and "One Hundred Views of Mount Fuji" will clarify the point.

In "Das Gemeine" the reader confronts Dazai as trickster. Both Dazai Osamu the author of the story and Dazai Osamu the author within the story offer off-the-cuff comments and show abrupt changes of conduct designed to catch a reader off guard. But one senses no *personal force* in the author of the story: one sees in the name Dazai Osamu within the story only a pattern of speech and behavior.

By contrast the Dazai of "One Hundred Views of Mount Fuji" makes the presence of his personality felt. As usual he is a devilish sort of character, privately mocking the "bride" and playing a trick on the simpering girls who want their picture taken. But the reader of "One Hundred Views of Mount Fuji" experiences these humorous occurrences through the personality of the author and for this reason comes away from the work knowing better what sort of person he has confronted in Dazai Osamu.

An exploration into the reasons for this difference would be an exercise for a subtle native critic. But one possible factor, to my knowledge yet unmentioned, is the presence in "One Hundred Views of Mount Fuji" of Japanese cultural traditions. Mount Fuji, with all its power of association and suggestion, looms large in the work. Writing in awareness of Hiroshige, Hokusai, and others, Dazai was able to escape the oppressive sense of his own self so prominent in a work like "Das Gemeine." If "One Hundred Views of Mount Fuji" were the only example of this combination (i.e., the escape from self-consciousness, the presence of light humor, and an awareness of traditions of some kind), the student of Dazai could probably overlook the matter. But other works, particularly the postwar *Tsugaru*, display a similar combination of elements. The notion that Dazai wrote autobiographically inspired work in a lighter vein only when he was working in awareness of Japanese tradition has much to recommend it.

And the works in this vein are, in my estimation, among the very best Dazai ever wrote. Why, it might be asked, did he not attempt more writings in this line? Perhaps Dazai himself did not regard a work like "One Hundred Views of Mount Fuji" very highly, or perhaps the comfortable relaxed style of life which gave rise to such a work was simply not to his liking.

In any event, the intention in his final four significant works of this period — "The Indictment," "Beggar-Student," "Run Melos," and *The New Hamlet* — differs considerably from "One Hundred Views of Mount Fuji." With the exception of "Beggar-Student," in these works Dazai turned from his own experience to well-known books for his basic story situation or even for the details of his plot. And, with this dependence on other sources, Dazai's outlook took on a moral tone more definite than that in any earlier works. Despite the ironies and ambiguities, these works readily yield fairly definite notions on such matters as money, friendship, and honesty in speech. Although I would not wish to push the correlation too far, it is almost as if Dazai, relieved of the bother of working out the basic plot structure, found the freedom to insert certain of his own moral ideas. The temptation to see Dazai's evolution in these terms becomes stronger during the next period of his career, the years of World War II. Dazai's important works during those years derive their plots even more closely than "Run Melos" or *The New Hamlet* from other literary works. And Dazai's major genre of writing during these war years might properly be called the "moral fable."

CHAPTER 4

The War Years (1941-1945)

I The Biography

THE outbreak of major hostilities with the United States
soon took away many of Dazai's friends. Ibuse Masuji was
sent to Singapore as a war correspondent; Dan Kazuo, after a period
of extended training in Japan, arrived in Manchuria where he
trekked about for a number of years. Dazai, too, was summoned for a
physical examination, but was rejected because of an ailing chest.
Left behind as old friends went off to war, Dazai found some consolation in the friendship of his Mitaka neighbor, the literary critic
Kamei Katsuichiro.

Kamei, a teetotaler, did not show any great enthusiasm for Dazai's
habit of appearing at his house regularly with some sake. Perhaps
Kamei's abstinence helped to keep Dazai's living style fairly steady
and regular during the course of the war. Dazai, in any event, continued to turn out stories in workmanlike fashion. Compelled like
other writers to avoid subjects of current controversy, he turned to
Japanese history and literature for much of his material. Although
circumstances forced this upon him to a degree, it must be noted
that he was in effect carrying on a line of work begun with such
earlier works as *The New Hamlet*.

In "The Fifteen Year Era," published in 1946, Dazai complained
rather bitterly about the severity of the wartime censorship. When
he added alongside the title of his novel *Sanetomo, Minister of the
Right* the phonetic reading "yu-da-ya-jin" (the Japanese for Jew),
the censor called him to order for treating the thirteenth-century
Japanese *shogun*-hero as a foreigner. Dazai, of course, merely
thought he was being witty. Certainly, his political innocence was
such that he probably did not foresee any difficulties in being
playful. Another work, which Dazai refers to simply as a "new novel
of over two-hundred pages," was not published until after the war.
Another shorter work was destroyed by order of the government cen-
sors.

Without meeting certain standards, then, Dazai could not get
published. Dazai neither put his feelings about the war in print nor

did he show much willingness to cooperate in the program of the Literature Patriotic Association. The government commissioned him to write a novel embodying patriotic ideals based on the life of the Chinese writer Lu Hsun. *Parting Regrets* failed as a novel and, as it was published only after the war, had no propaganda impact. As Donald Keene has pointed out: "It was incredible that Dazai, a writer lacking in political reliability or even citizenly virtues, should have been chosen to fulfill this patriotic task, and even more incredible that a work on Lu Hsun, a man associated with the resistance movement against Japan, should have been his subject."[1]

Dazai claimed in "The Fifteen Year Era" that he went on writing determinedly even when the censor refused publication. Yet he could not simply rest content with satisfying his creative urge. His wife bore two children during the war, and bounty from his home in Kanagi had long since ceased. Fortunately, his noncontroversial historical work found a market. During the war, by Keene's estimate, Dazai was the only Japanese writer who managed to get published and maintain his artistic integrity:

During the war Dazai alone continued to publish works of indisputable literary merit, and thereby encouraged young writers bored and disappointed by the propagandistic works — or else the silence — of other authors. Dazai's uncompromising devotion to his art, especially amidst the general paralysis of literature during the war, earned the admiration of the reading public.[2]

Despite the surface calm, Dazai was not completely free from anguish. As one might expect from the survivor of four suicide attempts, he showed little concern for his own physical safety. Indeed, by his own admission after the war, he again thought of committing suicide. Two considerations held him back. He thought the enemy might make a propaganda coup of his death. (Indeed, one sometimes gasps at the incredible illusions Dazai was subject to in thinking about himself.) More convincingly, he thought the news of his suicide would harm the morale of his friends fighting at the front. During the early stages of the war, the possibility of being drafted bothered him. Dazai, who owned no property, knew his departure would leave his wife penniless with a child — later, with two children — to care for. Oddly enough, he does not refer to their fate in contemplating the prospect of suicide.

Dazai remained with his family in Mitaka until March, 1945, when the bombing raids began to reach the suburbs of Tokyo. Dazai evacuated his wife and children to the home of his wife's parents in

Kofu, then returned to tend the house himself. But not for long. In April he too was living in Kofu, his home in Mitaka a charred ruin in the wake of an American fire raiding.

Dazai did not permit the fire raids to interfere with his writing. Crouched in the family air raid shelter, he entertained his daughter Sono — five years old in the final year of the war — and whiled away the tedium for himself by reading her Japanese fairy tales from a picture book. The stories captured his own imagination too, prompting him to retell them in his own terms. Within the year Dazai published a volume entitled *A Collection of Fairy Tales.* His personal feelings and opinions permeate his retelling of the stories, especially in the changes and additions to the source stories, but the works somehow survive as genuine fairy tales. Keene is exceptionally admiring:

Dazai's most perfect artistic creation may be *Otogi Zoshi.* He managed in his adaptation of these fairy tales, known in general outline to every Japanese child, to impart the characteristic Dazai flavor, normally associated with an extremely dark outlook on the world, without violating in any way the light-hearted spirit of the originals.[3]

Dazai's experience in fleeing American bombs was similar to Nagai Kafu's: he fled precisely where the bombs would strike next.[4] When Kofu was struck Dazai determined to flee with his family to Kanagi, his birthplace. Taking a large basket packed with rice-balls, they left Ueno Station by train after a long, dreary wait. Three days later — after several transfers, many delays, and such frightening sights as the bombed-out ruins of the station at Kooriyama — Dazai finally reached home. Shortly thereafter, bombs began to fall on Kanagi. But with no place to flee any longer, Dazai resigned himself: "If I'm going to be killed, I'll be lucky enough to die at home."[5]

Dazai's flight to Kanagi with his family might be considered a simple safety measure. Yet his own words suggest that he found peace at home, a surprising remark in view of his bitterness toward his home in the past.

Events during the war, however, had changed that. Previously, in 1941, at the insistence of a family acquaintance, Dazai had returned to Kanagi, apparently intent on using his newfound respectability to patch up the feud with his family. Shortly after his return to Tokyo, he was summoned back. His mother had fallen seriously ill and was on the brink of death. She clung to her life just long enough to allow her son time to return and bid her farewell.

Alienated during her life, Dazai and his mother were probably reconciled only in her death. At any rate, Dazai's attitude toward his home and its environs underwent a profound change. He voluntarily returned to Kanagi in January, 1943 — this time with his wife and daughter — for his mother's Buddhist memorial service. Then, in May of the following year, he was again off for Kanagi. The Koyama Publishing Company, planning a series to be entitled The New Fudoki Series,[6] commissioned Dazai to do the volume on the northernmost section of Honshu, the Tsugaru region.

From May 12 to June 5, Dazai traveled around to towns and villages he had never seen in his youth. The experience led to two results. One is the extremely charming record of his journey, *Tsugaru*. A second was his recognition of the worth of the Tsugaru native and his acceptance of himself as a crude farmer type in the very mold of the Tsugaru native. At the end of the war — especially in "The Fifteen Year Era" — he repeatedly insisted on this identity and on his utter contempt for the literary circle known in Japan as the "salon."[7] The reader of *Tsugaru* can easily accept Dazai's sentiment on reaching home near the end of the war that he would be happy to die in Kanagi.

II   A Retelling of the Tales from the Provinces

Although the title of this work is based on Ihara Saikaku's *Tales from the Provinces*, a collection of thirty-five stories published in 1685, only one of Dazai's twelve tales, "Stubborn in Poverty," is based on this particular Saikaku collection. The remainder are scattered throughout such other works by Saikaku as *The Eternal Storehouse of Japan* and *Tales of Warriors and Duty*.

The stories in *A Retelling of the Tales from the Provinces* were initially published in various magazines from January to November, 1944. The following January the entire collection was brought out under its present title by the Seikatsusha Publishing Company. In a short preface Dazai claimed that his works were not translations of Saikaku into modern Japanese — something he called a "meaningless exercise." Nevertheless, the adaptations from Saikaku are closer to the originals than the *Collection of Fairy Tales* he was to retell shortly. Okuno Tateo has conjectured that Dazai, who calls Saikaku in his preface the "world's greatest writer," was probably constrained by his great respect for Saikaku.[8]

This relative fidelity on Dazai's part results in a preservation of much of Saikaku's quality. Dazai successfully incorporates the social background and value clashes of the earlier stories, and even manages to capture something of Saikaku's quick wit and deft character typing.

III "Stubborn in Poverty"

The range of Dazai's selection suggests a wide acquaintance with Saikaku's work. His stated purpose in writing raises the question of why he chose these particular twelve stories out of such a great number — one story, for example, out of a total of thirty-five from Saikaku's Tales from the Provinces. "Stubborn in Poverty," the one selection from Tales from the Provinces, affords ample material for a comparative study between Dazai and his source. After giving a comparative analysis of these two tales, it will be well to briefly describe each tale, concentrating especially on those features of the narrative that might have prompted Dazai to choose it.

"Stubborn in Poverty," the first story in Dazai's collection, centers on a New Year's party given for his friends by a poor ronin, or masterless samurai, named Harada Naisuke. His samurai guests, as poor as he, have been invited to celebrate Harada's good fortune in receiving a gift of ten ryo from his brother-in-law, a doctor living near the Kanda Myojin shrine. At first Naisuke's seven guests are downcast. One of them confesses that he has gone so long without sake that he has forgotten how to drink; the others confess that they have forgotten how to get drunk. Nonetheless, once the guests understand that Naisuke has come into a windfall and will not charge them for the sake, they set about drinking with gusto. Once the party has livened up, Naisuke passes around the ten coins he has received. When they come back Naisuke finds one missing, but he is too timid to issue a challenge. After he finally reveals that one coin is missing, everyone, with a single exception, disrobes to prove that he has not stolen the coin. Eventually two coins turn up; the men discover one by the lamp stand, and Harada's wife finds another in the kitchen, stuck to the lid of a bowl from which the guests have been served. Naisuke is furious at this unexpected turn of events — he will not, despite his poverty, accept charity from his friends nor will he be made a fool of. When no one will admit to planting the extra coin, Naisuke works out a scheme whereby the owner may pick up his coin at the front door unseen.

Saikaku's original story, entitled "A New Year's Reckoning That Didn't Figure," is less elaborate than Dazai's retelling. Harada's brother-in-law, a doctor, sends a witty prescription in hopes of curing a case of poverty.[9] Finding himself the recipient of ten *ryo*, a "marvelous medicine" for curing countless ills, Harada invites seven of his samurai cronies to celebrate the windfall. After they arrive Harada passes the coins around, and finds one missing when they are returned to him. Two of the guests remove their sashes to show they have no money, but a third balks at putting himself to the test. Having just sold some goods he happens to have one *ryo* and some change on his person. He is on the verge of disemboweling himself when the missing coin is suddenly discovered in the shadow of the lamp stand. The appearance of the wife announcing the discovery of a second coin and Harada's stratagem for allowing the anonymous donor to get his *ryo* back without revealing his identity are basically the same in Saikaku's original as in Dazai's retelling.

Saikaku spins his yarn with characteristic brevity. He gives only an occasional glimpse of the characters he is portraying. The four or five opening lines of the tale suffice to tell the reader the basic facts of Harada Naisuke's existence: his lack of the necessities of life, his disheveled appearance, his threatening look as he makes an appeal to a rice-shop clerk. Harada the *ronin* has had to borrow a sword from the clerk, and he asks why he cannot keep it past the New Year into spring.

Saikaku packs his narrative tightly with brief details and shifts the focus of his tale from Harada to the brother-in-law to the seven friends and back to Harada with his customary speed and dexterity. Dazai, by contrast, is more concerned than Saikaku that the reader develop a definite conception of Naisuke. Dazai takes the poverty of Saikaku's Harada as an invitation to portray situations and responses recalling aspects of his own life. Describing the gift by the brother-in-law, he borrows Saikaku's witty pun, but — no doubt mindful of his own benefactors — he adds a touch of hauteur to the relatively benign figure of the brother-in-law in Saikaku. With Harada feigning insanity at the approach of New Year's Eve with its obligation to pay off all debts, his wife appeals to her doctor brother. The doctor's prescription, a "dose" of money, seems in the Dazai version a rather poor joke. Dazi implies that penurious souls like Harada (and himself) can readily be made fools of by their affluent relatives.

Harada, though, is not simply portrayed as the victim of his poverty. Departing radically from his source story, Dazai describes Harada refusing at first to accept charity. And, once he does accept, Harada feels an obligation to share his bounty with friends. No doubt Saikaku's Harada Naisuke is moved by similar feelings. Dazai, however, takes pains to make this feeling of obligation very explicit in his narrative.[10]

Saikaku, after briefly describing Harada's character, sets the plot moving and proceeds to the end without any delaying commentary. Dazai, on the contrary, is constantly tampering with Harada. As usual, Dazai is interested in the tale for its moral. Harada stands forth as the victim required by circumstances to accept charity, and as the plucky underdog who, within the limits possible to him, insists on his honor and dignity.

Despite the serious note, "Stubborn in Poverty" is very much a comic story. To read it in conjunction with Saikaku's tale provides insights into certain of Dazai's comic techniques. The economy of Saikaku's narrative style afforded Dazai a number of opportunities to rewrite or expand the original. In several instances Dazai, more conscious than Saikaku of the possibilities and demands of realism, creates in his characters a range of response wider than did Saikaku. Once the extra coin is discovered, the guests in Dazai's version bring forth the very plausible suggestion that Harada's brother-in-law might have added the extra coin just for fun. In Saikaku, on the other hand, the guests are silent on this question.

Again Dazai spells out meanings that are only implicit in the Saikaku narrative. In Saikaku, once it becomes clear that the owner of the extra coin will not reveal himself, Harada simply says that he will place a measuring box with the coin inside on the garden wash basin. The guests are to leave one by one; thus, the owner of the coin will be able to pick it up in private.

In his closing scene, Dazai is very explicit about making it difficult for the other six guests to gather any hints in leaving as to who the owner of the coin might be. Dazai's Harada says: "If we put the coin at the edge of the step in the darkest place, no one will be able to see whether or not it's there. The owner of the coin alone is to feel around with his hand, then go out as if nothing were amiss."[11]

The interesting aspect of this is not the idle question of which version is more effective or foolproof. Rather, the reader should simply be aware of the double irony involved in Dazai's reordering of Saikaku. For Saikaku himself had taken similar liberties as an author, writing parodies of earlier Japanese literature with such titles as *Nise Monogatari* and *The "Gay" Tale of the Heike*.[12] Saikaku even tampered with the best of classical Japanese fiction. The fifty-four chapters of *The Man Who Spent His Life in Love* parallel the fifty-four chapters of *The Tale of Genji;* the multiple sordid adventures of Saikaku's hero Yonosuke parody the Genji tradition of high romance.

Dazai's intentions, then, in writing "Stubborn in Poverty" involve certain aspects of his own life and the possibilities he saw in the Saikaku original for the application of comic techniques of style. That he wrote about the *ronin* so soon after describing Minamoto Sanetomo in his historical novel, *Sanetomo, Minister of the Right*, reveals Dazai's continued interest in the relation of the samurai ethic to life.

Dazai could also have been drawn to the original tale by the ambiguity inherent in Saikaku's narrative method. Readers of the several excellent English translations of Saikaku's *koshokubon*, or erotic works, will realize the difficulty of determining the author's attitude toward events and characters he describes. In *Five Women Who Loved Love*, for example, Saikaku's characters often fall in love in ways that violate social law and custom only to meet "justice" ultimately on the execution ground.[13] In these cases, Saikaku appears to sanction the harsh penalties of the Tokugawa code; at the same time, he describes the illicit love affair with such gusto that no reader can believe he is absolutely condemning his lovers.

A similar ambiguity exists in Saikaku's "New Year's Reckoning That Didn't Figure." The subject of Saikaku's work is listed as *giri*, or obligation. But the reader, having finished the tale, is less than certain of Saikaku's feelings. "In the quick wit of the host, the behavior of his familiar guests, indeed in many ways the relations among the samurai are different [i.e., from those of the townsmen]," Saikaku declares, ending his tale. But, as so often happens in Saikaku, the final moral comment can hardly obliterate the import of the narrative. One feels with Saikaku that the samurai are rather foolish in their insistence on dignity. Why should the mere sum of one *ryo* create such havoc? Why should a man under suspicion by his friends for a petty crime ready his sword to take his life? Surely the merchants and townsmen who read Saikaku found such behavior strange.[14]

Shortly before he began his *Retelling of the Tales from the Provinces*, Dazai had expressed his admiration for the samurai virtues in *Sanetomo, Minister of the Right*. In "Stubborn in Poverty" he examines the lives of *ronin* at the very bottom of the samurai class. If the *shogun* Sanetomo represents an ideal, the *ronin* in "Stubborn in Poverty" perhaps represent what is amiss with the ethic of the warrior. Or, rather, they represent attitudes and behavior of noble samurai diminished (perhaps to the point of absurdity) by the poverty in which these men now find themselves. As usual, the reader of Dazai finds it difficult to pin down his elusive,

ironic author. Surely Dazai saw something noble in the samurai virtues; perhaps he felt that these were the sole virtues that could survive the war. Regardless of whether he looked foolish or pompous, a
man ought to cling to such a heritage.

IV "Great Strength"

The second tale, a thin piece entitled "Great Strength" and taken
from Saikaku's *Twenty-four Instances of Unfilial Conduct in Our
Country,* details the feats of a sumo wrestler, Saibei. An uncouth
youth given to beating up other people, Saibei is urged by his father
to try his hand at other sports, football, for example, or even flower
arrangement. His mother, hoping to plant in him the seeds of compassion, persuades him to take a bride. Unfortunately, as Saibei
reveals to his wife on their wedding night, he has taken a vow to the
god Marishiten never to touch a woman. The story ends abruptly
when Waniguchi, Saibei's old wrestling tutor, defeats his ex-pupil in
a wrestling match by a clever stratagem. Dazai was prompted to
retell the story, one might imagine, to capitalize on the opportunities
for wit and humor it afforded at a number of points.

V "The Monkey's Grave"

The third tale, "The Monkey's Grave," is drawn from *The
Inkstone of Nostalgia* and is clearly Dazai's kind of story. As in the
case of "Great Strength," Dazai was doubtless intrigued by the comic potential of "The Monkey's Grave." Jiroemon dispatches a friend
to talk to the father of his beloved Oran about arranging a marriage.
The father is anxious that Oran, brought up in the Nichiren Buddhist sect, marry a fellow believer, and he immediately traps the
hapless go-between into admitting ignorance of Jiroemon's religion.
Then, to make matters worse, the go-between blurts out that this
makes no difference; Jiroemon, regardless of his present beliefs, can
always convert to Nichiren. Condemning this opportunism, Oran's
father reveals that he has already betrothed her to another, a firm
Nichiren believer.

Oran and Jiroemon, taking matters into their own hands, decide to
elope. At this point in the story enters Dazai's favorite animal, a
monkey.

This monkey, named Kichibei, was so attached to Oran it hobbled off in pursuit the night she ran away with a strange man. When Jiroemon and Oran
had covered about three miles, the girl noticed her pet. Though she scolded
and pelted him with stones, the monkey limped along after her. Finally,

Jiroemon took pity. "He's followed you this far. Let him join us."
"Here boy," Oran beckoned and the monkey came bounding. As she hugged him the monkey looked mournfully at his two companions and blinked his eyes.[15]

After Oran and Jiroemon settle in a humble cottage, Kichibei helps about the house. With the birth of a son, Kikunosuke, the monkey becomes a baby-sitter.

The story comes to a tragic end, though, just as Oran and Jiroemon are laying plans to return to society to give Kikunosuke the advantages of a respectable upbringing. They leave Kichibei to tend the baby while they go off to discuss a business deal with a neighboring farmer.

In a little while Kichibei recalled it was time for the infant's bath. So he lit a fire under the stove to boil some water — precisely, he recalled, as Oran always did.
When bubbles started to rise Kichibei poured the steaming water into a basin to the very rim. Without bothering to test the water he stripped the child naked, lifted him, and — peering into his face in imitation of Oran — gently dipped the child two or three times in the basin.
"Waa!" The parents, hearing the shrill cry of the scalded baby, glanced at each other and came running back to the house. The stunned Kichibei stood transfixed as the baby floated about the basin. Oran, lifting the corpse, could scarcely bear the sight of this "broiled lobster."[16]

The hysterical Oran tries to kill Kichibei, but Jiroemon intervenes to save the monkey.
One hundred days after the infant's death, Kichibei, standing on the new grave, takes his own life in atonement. Oran and Jiroemon bury him sadly; they have forgiven him the crime he committed in his animal innocence and have come to realize that, after the baby's death, Kichibei is the only thing they have.

Kichibei, then, is one of a considerable group of symbolic monkeys in Dazai's works. Kichibei represents a Dazai ideal: unselfish service to the interest of another. At the same time, his innocence causes him to blunder in such a way that his ideals, like the author's, bring destruction and sorrow.

VI   "Mermaid Sea"

The following tale, taken from Saikaku's *A Record of Traditions of the Warrior's Way,* is entitled "Mermaid Sea." Like *Sanetomo,*

Minister of the Right, "Mermaid Sea" is an expression of certain samurai virtues.

A boat encounters a freak storm on the ocean. Everyone aboard gradually loses consciousness, with the exception of the virtuous samurai Chudo Konnai. When a mermaid appears in the waves, he shoots her with an arrow. She sinks, the storm subsides, and Chudo's companions regain consciousness.

When a report of this feat is made to the regional lord, one of the samurai in attendance expresses disbelief. Aozaki, the samurai in question, is described by Dazai as a good-for-nothing who holds a high official position only by virtue of the exploits of his father. But so forcefully does Aozaki express his contempt toward wondrous events that the other samurai present at the occasion become utterly bewildered. Chudo, in true samurai fashion, will not rest with his word called into question. He organizes a search of the area of the sea where the slaying occurred. Yet, when a thorough search uncovers no evidence of his feat, he begins himself to doubt the event.

At this point, the narrative switches to Chudo's house, where his daughter and her attendant are growing restless and concerned over his safety. Finally, they set out in search, only to find his corpse on the beach wrapped in seaweed. A samurai follower of Chudo's arrives on horseback. He dismisses the entire question of the truth or falsity of Chudo's account and charges the daughter to avenge her father by killing Aozaki. The latter is guilty of slandering and sending him to his death. The daughter kills Aozaki and marries a young samuari, who takes the name Chudo in order to carry on the dead man's family name. Finally, for good measure, the skeleton of a mermaid, with Chudo's arrowhead embedded in the shoulder blade, is washed ashore.

VII   *"Bankruptcy"*

In paying deference to Saikaku in his preface to *A Retelling of the Tales from the Provinces,* Dazai added the caveat that, for him, Saikaku's series of erotic stories were not to his taste. But, of course, this was Saikaku's métier, and most Japanese readers today, as well as Westerners who have read him in translation, associate Saikaku with this series of works.

The next two stories, "Bankruptcy" and "Naked in the River," deal with another important concern of Saikaku — money. "Bankruptcy" comes from the collection treating the crafty practices of the Osaka merchant, *The Eternal Storehouse of Japan.* "River of the Naked," along with the next tale, "Obligation," is taken from *Tales of the Knightly Code of Honor.*

"Bankruptcy" slyly narrates the downfall of the prosperous house of Yorozuya. The owner of the family business is a self-made man of nearly fanatical thrift. Fearing for the future of the business, he disinherits his effeminate son and adopts in his stead a young man whose thrifty habits appear to guarantee continued prosperity for the house. With admirable foresight the adopted son recommends that a jealous woman be found for him to marry. The hard opposition of a shrew will protect him from the temptation so common among the merchants of Tokugawa Japan of squandering the family fortune in the pleasure quarter.

Unfortunately the wife proves to be such a killjoy that her husband is soon looking for relief. When his foster parents die, he leaves for Kyoto and squanders his fortune in a year. Returning home he sets to work rebuilding the family business in hopes of returning to Kyoto for another round of fun. Concealing his actual penury, he operates a thriving brokerage simply on the appearance of wealth. Before he can recoup his fortune, an accident upsets his well-laid plans. One New Year's Eve, the night for clearing all debts, a poor *ronin* enters his office demanding change to pay off a trifling debt. The broker does not have the money to make the transaction, and so small is the amount that he cannot plead that he is short of ready cash. The poor *ronin*'s cry of surprise informs the neighbors that the apparently prosperous business is in fact bankrupt.

VIII *"River of the Naked"*

The opening scene of "River of the Naked" shows an official of the Kamakura Bakufu named Aotosaemon transporting government funds across a river. Opening the money pouch, he accidentally drops eleven coins into the river. Although the loss represents a small sum, Aotosaemon hires at considerable expense to himself a group of peasants who search the river for the missing coins.

One of the searchers, a scoundrel named Asada, has hired on simply to share in the reward. Bored with the search and aware that the subsidy from Aotosaemon greatly exceeds the value of the lost coins, Asada decides to conclude matters by pretending to find the coins. Deceiving his companions, he pretends to probe the river bottom with his foot as he surreptitiously slips the requisite coins from his own sash.

While the peasants celebrate the find with a banquet, Aotosaemon returns home and happily reports to his family the details of the incident. Suddenly he is taken aback by a remark of his daughter. She reminds him that he was carrying two coins fewer than usual, and thus his original calculation that eleven coins had fallen into the river must be revised.

Enraged, Aotosaemon returns to the river and compels Asada to search alone for the money, insisting that he stay in the river until every missing coin is recovered. Asada emerges on the ninety-seventh day, having turned up, in addition to the coins, numerous articles people have lost or discarded in the river over the years. His task finished, Asada unabashedly demands from Aotosaemon the eleven "counterfeit" coins.

IX *"Obligation"*

In his next selection from Saikaku, Dazai again portrays a man willing to carry out unhesitatingly an action imposed on him by the dictates of a feudal society. In this instance Dazai's protagonist is a samurai compelled by obligation to sacrifice his innocent son.

The villains and heroes are clearly marked in this work. Muramaro, the son of an important lord of the province of Settsu, decides on a whim to make a journey to the distant northern island of Hokkaido. To accompany his son, the lord chooses a varied group of men from among his followers. A trusted samurai named Kamizaki Shikibu is to oversee the journey; Kamizaki's son Katsutaro, along with a youth named Tanzaburo, are designated to make the trip as companions to the son of the lord. Like his father Shikibu, Katsutaro is a model samurai; Tanzaburo, the son of an official associated with Shikibu, is lazy and pleasure loving.

As the group heads north, progress is delayed by the carousing habits of Tanzaburo and the young lord. Each night, at a different inn, the two youths stay up late feasting and reveling with the serving-maids. Mornings they remain slugabed, while the members of the retinue idly await their pleasure.

Eventually the travelers reach the Oi River, which empties into the Pacific midway between Kyoto and Tokyo. Kamizaki Shikibu, responsible for the general welfare, counsels that the group pass the night at a nearby inn and attempt the difficult crossing the following morning. But the young lord, impetuous by nature, urges an immediate crossing; spurred on by the thoughtless Tanzaburo, the young lord fords the treacherous stream on horseback. Tanzaburo begins to regret his role in calling for an immediate crossing the moment his own turn arrives. Although Shikibu and Katsutaro try to guide their charge carefully, Tanzaburo falls from his saddle and disappears in the current.

As soon as Kamizaki Shikibu reaches the shore, he orders his son Katsutaro to drown himself in the river. Prior to the journey, Kamizaki had guaranteed to Tanzaburo's father the safety of the son. Once the pledge is broken, Kamizaki, in true samurai fashion, demands of himself the same loss inflicted on the father of Tanzaburo.

When the entourage finally returns to Settsu, Kamizaki and his wife exile themselves from society to pray for the salvation of Katsutaro. Hearing of Shikibu's sacrifice, the father of Tanzaburo is impelled to leave society with his family and likewise pray for the salvation of the unfortunate Katsutaro.

X *"Female Bandits"*

Most of the works in Dazai's *A Retelling of the Tales from the Provinces* have a rural setting. Occasionally a story has both a rural and an urban setting. "Female Bandits" is one of these latter tales; it is also the only story in the collection to explicitly contrast urban and rural values.

A prosperous bandit from the northern region of Sendai arrives at the capital of Kyoto to amuse himself. Though uncouth, he gains a considerable reputation throughout the town as a liberal spender. One day he catches sight of an attractive girl and falls immediately in love. Overwhelming the girl's greedy father with munificent gifts, the bandit wins the girl as his bride and takes her off to Sendai.

At first the girl is appalled at the barbarism of life in the north; she is also shocked to discover the source of her husband's prosperity. Within a short time, however, she becomes accustomed to her new life. After giving birth to two girls, she sees to it that both are brought up wise in the methods of brigandage.

When the daughters reach late adolescence, their father is crushed to death in an avalanche of snow. At first, there is some argument as to whether the two daughters, with help from their mother, can continue their dangerous and demanding way of life.

Eventually a strange turn of events brings their operation to a halt. Having divided a stolen fabric, each sister concocts a secret scheme to kill the other. Disillusioned with the uncouth ways of Sendai, each sister has begun yearning for a feminine mode of life. Each sister wants the other's fabric to make herself a lined kimono.

Before anything drastic can occur, the younger sister breaks into tears and begs forgiveness. Having caught sight of smoke rising from a nearby crematorium, she has suddenly come to realize the vanity and evanescence of human life. The elder sister, needless to say, makes a similar confession and asks forgiveness. Thereupon the two sisters, in the company of their mother, renounce the world and take up a life of prayer in expiation for the misdeeds of their past.

XI *"The Great Red Drum"*

Tokubei, a weaver in the Nishijin area of Kyoto, has always been an industrious worker and upright person. Despite his good qualities, he seems destined to live out his life in poverty. While the other weaving establishments carry on a thriving business, Tokubei's remains close to bankruptcy.

When it becomes known throughout Nishijin that Tokubei will be hard pressed to meet his debts at year's end, ten of his peers agree to donate ten *ryo* apiece in hopes of giving the worthy man the start he needs. They deliver the money to Tokubei's house and celebrate the occasion with a boisterous party. After the guests depart, Tokubei and his wife discover that the money is also gone. Despondent over the loss, the couple decide to put an end to their misfortunes.

Tokubei's wife adorned herself in the white kimono she had managed to keep despite their poverty. Then, facing the mirror to comb down the black hair people had praised from her childhood, she mourned her nineteen years of conjugal intimacy suddenly reduced to a mere predawn dream.
She composed herself and gently woke her two children. The older child, a girl, mumbled drowsily: "Is it New Year's, Mommy?" The younger, a boy, asked whether she would buy him a top today.
Blinded by tears Tokubei and his wife set the children without a word before the alter. Holding aloft the vigil lamps with their quivering flames, each member of the family joined his hand in prayer to the ancestral spirits.[17]

In the nick of time a nursemaid rushes in to put a stop to the proceedings. When word of the theft spreads in the neighborhood, the famous Judge Itakura is called in to solve the crime.

His solution is ingenious. After narrowing the number of suspects to a group of ten men, he decrees that each suspect, with the assistance of his nearest female relative, must carry a large red drum from his office to the Hachiman shrine and back. Ten days later, when each couple has carried the drum once, Itakura assembles the suspects:

Now among this group there is one woman who, upon entering the cedar forest with the great drum, raised such an insane racket she seemed to be possessed by a devil. One by one she brought up her husband's past blunders, while he tried in vain to calm her. So nettled did the husband grow at the increasing clamor that, as they emerged from the forest into the field, he counseled her in a hushed voice: "Calm down please. If we can persevere in this nasty chore, the one hundred *ryo* will be ours. When we return home take a look in the chest of drawers."

Surely the speaker remembers his own strange words. The gods didn't inform on him. But the young acolyte I ordered to hide inside the drum heard all and reported back to me. Now you know why that red drum was so heavy.[13]

XII   *"The Refined Man"*

Dazai wrote several stories between the end of World War II and his death in 1948 that seem to reflect his awareness that he was not fulfilling his role as a husband and father. Typically these stories depict a man squandering his income while his wife remains at home trying to meet her household responsibilities as best she can. The present story, "The Refined Man," might well be considered the first in this thematic series of tales.

It is the last day of the year, that favored day in Saikaku's writings when all debts must be cleared. Dazai's "Refined Man" departs early from home, leaving his wife with only a few inadequate coins to meet the crowd of anticipated creditors. Arriving at one of the few teahouses where he is unknown, the protagonist presents himself as a wealthy patron looking for a place to pass the time. He tells the teahouse matron that his wife is expected to bear a child this very day, and that the people attending her have chased him from home.

The matron, wise in the ways of the world, sees through this tale, but goes along with his pretension. She serves up a boiled egg and a plate of herring roe, along with several cups of sake. With the help of an aging geisha, the matron soon relieves the "Refined Man" of his paltry fortune.

Unable to maintain the pretense of wealth any longer, the man dismisses the geisha and stretches out on the floor of the teahouse parlor to sleep through the rest of the day. Presently two henchmen burst in to admonish him for wasting the money he owes his creditors. They strip him of his jacket, kimono, and sword. Left with only his underwear, the "Refined Man" fabricates an outlandish explanation for the intrusion and insists on remaining in the teahouse until evening in order to leave unseen.

XIII   *"Admonition"*

"Admonition" describes an adventure of three young dandies from Kyoto. Bored with the pleasures of their own city, the dandies journey in search of new amusements to Edo, the city that developed into modern Tokyo. At first they find Edo little different from Kyoto. Eventually, however, their attention is drawn to a store where goldfish are sold for considerable sums. Awestruck, the three friends do not recognize in the seedy fellow selling mosquito larvae for goldfish food their bosom friend of earlier days, Tsukiyo no Risa. The latter, who has recognized his old cronies, tries to slip away unnoticed, but, before he can escape, the three dandies catch up with him and begin railing at his aloofness.

Tsukiyo no Risa invites his old friends to a wretched tavern and treats them to drinks with the money he has just earned selling larvae. Eventually the four companions wend their way to Tsukiyo no Risa's house, where the three Kyoto blades renew another old acquaintanceship. Once an attractive Kyoto geisha, Tsukiyo no Risa's wife Kichishu is now a careworn housewife with four "monkey-faced" boys to look after. Appalled by the squalor of Tsukiyo no Risa's life, the three friends surreptitiously leave behind some money as they depart from the house. Their friend stubbornly refuses such charity and leaves shortly thereafter for the countryside with his family. The three dandies return home, vowing to amend their lives. The sight of an old friend fallen into misfortune has served as a reproach to their own carefree, luxurious mode of life.

XIV *"Mount Yoshino"*

A young man, for reasons never precisely disclosed, has rejected society and exiled himself deep in the Yoshino Hills of Nara Prefecture. Confessing that his action was rash and regrettable, the hermit writes an old friend lamenting his exile and imploring certain favors.

The harsh demands of a solitary life in the wild have obliterated the vague romantic notions that seem to have prompted the move into exile. Mentioning an aristocratic poem which "elegantly confuses" snow on a bush with the eagerly awaited spring flowers, the writer bitterly complains that, for him, snow is simply snow. He reserves even harsher criticism for the peasants and farmers in the vicinity. By the hermit's reckoning, these scoundrels are out to gouge him for the simple necessities he must buy just to survive.

In the course of the letter, he confesses his desire to return to society. But several considerations prevent such a move, particularly the thought of his fearsome grandmother who might have already discovered that he has stolen her cache of money. After asking his correspondent to carry out several transactions, the hermit brings his letter to a close on an uncertain note. Unable to return to society, he expresses the hope that his acquaintances will see their way to paying him a visit in the spring.

XV   A Retelling of the Tales from the Provinces *in Retrospect*

The hermit in "Mount Yoshino" is the closest figure in the collection to what might be termed a Dazai surrogate. In general, the stories depict outgoing people active within their respective societies. The brooding, withdrawn figure so common in Dazai's earlier works is almost nonexistent in the world of Saikaku.

This is not to imply that Dazai, in choosing to recreate Saikaku, misjudged the nature of his own talent. Quite the contrary, for some of the finest passages in *A Retelling of the Tales from the Provinces* — the drinking scene in "Stubborn in Poverty" with its gruff camaraderie, for example — represent social activities. And Dazai, it must be added, was not simply borrowing Saikaku's deft skill at colloquial, idiomatic dialogue. In his next important work, *Tsugaru*, Dazai utilized his own talent for dialogue to vividly re-create scenes of nostalgic camaraderie he experienced himself on a trip through the region of his birth. Indeed, in reading *Tsugaru*, one almost feels that Saikaku has taught Dazai to relax and enjoy himself in the company of others. The priggish Dazai of "Beggar-Student" is nowhere in evidence in *Tsugaru*.

On another plane Dazai conceivably sought in Saikaku some kind of religious or ethical guidance. Readers familiar with Saikaku's superficial treatment of certain moral and religious problems of early Tokugawa Japan may well question such a suggestion. It is nonetheless remarkable how often religion plays a momentary but crucial role in *A Retelling of the Tales from the Provinces*. Consider, for example, Waniguchi's monkish guise in "Great Strength," the religious obstacle to the marriage proposed in "The Monkey's Grave," the Buddhistic sense of life's emptiness in the final scene of "Female Bandits," the moral lesson of a friend's decline in "Admonition," the sense of futility at leading the purest kind of religious life in "Mount Yoshino." And a careful search will begin to uncover here and there in the collection Dazai's own moral notions presented as a natural expression of character or plot. One recalls Naisuke in "Stubborn in Poverty," ready to claim a right precisely when it goes against his self-interest, or the monkey Kichibei in "The Monkey's Grave," unselfishly carrying out a service which becomes a disaster for those he would serve. The brooding Dazai surrogate may be missing, but the style and the "ideas in disguise" reveal the author behind these tales.

Above all, Dazai possibly saw many of the characters of *A Retelling of the Tales from the Provinces* as examples of simplicity in the face of complex urbanity, and frugality in the face of extravagance. Such themes are especially evident in "Bankruptcy," "River of the Naked," and "Obligation," where the simple demands and prompt, virtuous actions of samurai figures contrast with the deceptive and selfish behavior of the commoners, the merchants, and the pampered higher nobility. A sophisticated contemporary reader might criticize Dazai for seeking anything other than the entertainment values of good narrative in the world of Saikaku; but it seems likely that Dazai saw in such virtues as frugality and simplicity a bulwark against the self-destructive conduct of his youth. In this sense *A Retelling of the Tales from the Provinces* reaffirms the resolution that Dazai voiced on the occasion of his marriage to Ishihara Michiko to develop his talents in pursuit of a useful life.

XVI   Tsugaru

Dazai, at first glance, does not seem a likely writer to compose a book on the history and customs of a given area, particularly a book intended to form part of a series of such works by various authors. Dazai is above all an idiosyncratic writer whose feelings and moods constitute his main subject. However, toward the end of the war, writers of stature with leisure and a claim to personal knowledge of the Tsugaru region must have been scarce. Perhaps Dazai received the commission in default of any other candidate.

Not that Dazai himself, as he engagingly points out several times in *Tsugaru*, knew much himself about the region of his birth and upbringing. Naturally he had some knowledge of Kanagi, his hometown; of Aomori, where he attended middle school; and of Hirosaki, where he went to higher school. Yet he seldom traveled anywhere in the region before he went to Tokyo. And the youthful writings show that he was more introspective and less aware of his physical environment as a youth than he was as an adult.

Accordingly, to write an honest book, Dazai had to study and travel. As one might surmise, he does not wear his scholarship lightly. He tends to overquote his authorities — as though this were a requirement of the genre — without making any effort to integrate their findings with his own personal, and very sharp, observations.

He quotes mainly in the hope of supporting what he would like to believe about Tsugaru. An Ainu people were the earliest inhabitants of the area; but, unlike the usual breed now in Hokkaido, the old Tsugaru Ainu was an industrious fellow. Dazai interprets the fact that there was much movement and migration in the area to mean that the natives were not idlers. Perhaps he was imagining the past on the basis of what he observed in the present. He was, for example, immensely impressed with the vigor of the natives in villages along the sea coast fighting both the sea and the weather for survival.

The reader, then, must approach Dazai's Tsugaru "history" with caution. At the same time, the reader cannot avoid a mild shock at how far Dazai has discarded certain attitudes of his youth. Then, Tsugaru was a culturally barren, inferior place. It had done nothing for his ancestors, nor for him. The only previous time Dazai ever attached a positive value to his birthplace was in imagining it — in "Landlord for a Generation," for example — as the scene of a possible democratic revolution.

Conceivably, premonitions of his own death could have prompted this remarkable change in attitude. Dazai, we have seen, had again contemplated suicide during the war, and he might have guessed that bombs would soon be falling on Tokyo. Furthermore, Dazai — who obviously liked to imagine himself in the company of the great and famous — discovered a new group in that conspicuously large number of modern Japanese writers (Kitamura Tokoku, Arishima Takeo, Akutagawa Ryunosuke) who committed suicide on (or slightly past) the threshold of middle age.

Absent from his home almost entirely for over a decade, Dazai thought this might be his final return to Tsugaru. Whether his attitude changed in looking forward to his return home, or as a consequence of his experiences once he had arrived, is unclear. But, for whatever reasons, the metropolis became the den of sin and iniquity corrupting innocents who wandered in from far-flung places like Kanagi. His old Tsugaru self — past feelings and judgments to the contrary — became a virtuous figure. He and his old friend "N" had both been generous boys, trusting even the deceitful. "N" had gone to work for an insurance company in Tokyo; fortunately he had returned to Tsugaru before corruption set in. Dazai discovers him on his junket — still a man of "pure character," while he himself has "gradually turned into a somber, mean character."[19]

Accordingly, Dazai determines to fight against the influence of the city. He declares that he is still a rough farmer sprung from the Tsugaru soil and that the city has merely put a veneer over him. In his own words, "As a city dweller I have many anxieties; I hope to find the native of Tsugaru in myself."[20]

In the later pages of *Tsugaru* he seems momentarily to have found his native self. In a moving account of his reunion with the old nursemaid Take, Dazai proclaims the great pride he takes in the fact that a peasant woman nursed him.

As always, Dazai's reversals and contradictions are easy to detect. Still, as far as his development as an artist is concerned, one readily feels that he has instinctively made the right choice in treating Tsugaru as he does. The dull passages in the work are almost all quotations from the work of others. One likes to think they were brought in grudgingly, a necessary concession to the genre Dazai had committed himself to.

The notion of returning to Tsugaru in search of something sharpened Dazai's sensitivity to events. A perfect example of this heightened awareness of his environment is the final episode of the work, by implication the most important of the many searches in Tsugaru. Dazai vividly records each step in the hunt for his old nursemaid Take, conveying to his reader as he proceeds a sense of his own excitement and suspense.

He searches first among the crowd watching an athletic meet. After circulating several times through the crowd, he decides to go to the hardware store which, he has learned, Take now manages. But the shop is closed, its front door locked. He turns away in despair, only to return shortly and find the padlock off the door. Entering, Dazai finds Take's daughter and persuades her to take him to her mother. Dazai's reunion with Take occurs at the athletic meet. Since they exchange only a few words and turn to watch the events, the scene in itself, especially in English translation, gives no sense of its real impact. The restraint of the description tells only insofar as it comes immediately upon the excitement and suspense of the search.

In the midst of the satisfaction he feels in Take's presence, Dazai experiences one faint regret: "I think I can say that I experienced at that moment genuine peace for the first time in my life. My deceased mother was a fine, gentle woman; but she never gave me such a marvelous sense of peace."[21] The mild resentment is less crucial to the student of Dazai than the admission that his mother was a woman of quality.

Dazai in fact treated both his parents in the same "unhistorical" manner in which he treated Tsugaru. He nullified certain earlier slanders by pointing out that he was a mere fourteen when his father died. Recently he had been having fantastic dreams about his father. Then the old revolutionary who would provoke revolt among the peasants against the oppression exercised by a father-landlord declared: "If my father had lived longer he probably would have accomplished some great work for the benefit of Tsugaru."[22] Dazai's first act upon entering the family home at Kanagi is to pay his respects before the likenesses of his parents at the family altar. Later in the narrative, when he visits his father's birthplace in a neighboring town, he realizes with a start that the plans his father was making at the time of his death to renovate the house in Kanagi were an attempt to make that house resemble his birthplace. For the first time the thought of his father as an individual with certain tastes and desires strikes Dazai.

This reversal of opinion involved a second reversal of his earlier idea of the uncompromising nature of fate. Although a few passages in *Tsugaru* hint that he has not rid himself of defeatism, the dominant tone is optimistic. Even when, in rare somber moments, he admits that his ancestors were inferior, Dazai affirms that he is responsible to them: "A person has just one option: that is, to develop himself as far as he can within the limits heredity has imposed upon him."[23]

Dazai's heightened awareness of his environment resulted in some of his most brilliant character sketches. The author's old friend "S" invites him home for food and drinks. As they enter, "S" announces Dazai's arrival, bawls for sake, then sends his wife packing for two extra bottles when he can find only one in the house. He demands that she wait a minute, then sends her off again to get dried cuttlefish besides the sake. Before she can get out of the house, he has added soy sauce to the list, as well as apple wine and sugar. On her way out she is ordered to turn on the phonograph, then to turn it off so the host and his guest needn't shout to be heard. The narration is handled so well that the reader imagines for himself the harassed wife, who is never actually described.[24]

"S," who appears in the first half of *Tsugaru*, gives Dazai his first experience of native hospitality. Dazai is especially impressed by the "naturalness" of his friend's behavior, particularly in contrast to his own clumsiness in welcoming and entertaining guests in his own home. In part this is a repetition of the "country innocence" theme; "S" has remained in Tsugaru and, like the natives Dazai encounters during the remainder of the journey, has no complexes or defenses isolating him from his fellow man. In the presence of such innocence, Dazai's own chronic self-consciousness is relatively quiescent. He feels inferior to "S" on a specific point for a particular reason. The vague fears and unprovoked worries of many other autobiographical works creep into *Tsugaru* only occasionally.

A final conspicuous point in *Tsugaru* is Dazai's numerous references to the famous seventeenth-century haiku poet Basho. Perhaps setting out on what he thought might be a final, decisive journey — a pilgrimage, in a sense — turned Dazai's mind to Basho. One recalls Basho late in life selling his house in Edo and, like Dazai, setting out for the "Deep North" on a search.[25]

Surprisingly, Dazai does not advert to the parallelism. Rather, he contrasts Basho's humility — he quotes the poet's motto "Raise others and humble yourself" — with his own practice of slandering his fellow writers. Again he praises Basho's break with convention. (Here Dazai probably considered himself an innovator along with Basho.) These comments on Basho follow immediately upon Dazai's hearing a carp jumping in a pond and proposing, on the basis of this experience, a new interpretation of the famous haiku on the old pond and the frog. Dazai dismissed the "schoolroom" explanation of a quiet, dark afternoon broken by the momentary sound and followed by the relapse into silence. He thought the atmosphere was bright, the sound of the water a playful splash.

XVII   A Collection of Fairy Tales: *"Taking the Wen"*

The first of Dazai's four tales is entitled "Taking the Wen." In his introductory comments to this tale, Dazai records his belief that the earliest extant text is that contained in the thirteenth-century collection *Tales from Uji*. Evidently Dazai read to his daughter during the war from one of the children's editions of fairy tales, editions which generally rework the original story in a simple, colloquial style.

The *Uji* text of "Taking the Wen" is vague about the domestic situation of the main character, an old firewood gatherer. The first paragraph, after mentioning the wen on the man's right cheek, moves quickly to a description of a storm that detains the wood gatherer in the forest one day. Hiding in the hollow of a tree, the old man notices a swarm of hideous demons gathering nearby. The demons drink themselves into a merry state, and presently each is in turn performing his favorite dance. So entranced by their spirit is the old man that he ventures forth to perform the most exciting dance of all.

The demons ask the old man to return another day to dance; to guarantee his return, they take the wen from his cheek as a kind of security. Thereupon the wood gatherer returns home and reveals the adventure to his wife and neighbor. The neighbor, an old man with a wen on his left cheek, decides to have his wen removed in the same way. But he dances so poorly that the demons decide to attach the first man's wen to the right cheek of the second. A moral, appended at the end of the tale, cautions against envy.

Dazai expands the tale considerably. As in his adaptation of Saikaku's "Stubborn in Poverty," he makes the action of "Taking the Wen" more diverse and the characters more complex. He describes at length the old wood gatherer, a mediocre man with a cold, efficient wife and a virtuous prig of a son. The old man seems impelled to drink as a cure for loneliness; with no friends whatever, he is reduced to regarding the wen on his cheek as the focus of his affections.

In Dazai's version the wood gatherer goes forth to dance in front of the demons, emboldened by an evening of solitary drinking. The demons are again so pleased by the dance that they take the wen to assure the old man's return. Upon his arrival at home, only the neighbor with the wen on his left cheek seems interested in the old man's adventure. As in the original, the neighbor enters the woods in hopes of having his wen removed, only to end up with a wen on both cheeks.

Dazai's alterations of the original tale tend to underline the theme of camaraderie. The wood gatherer is not depicted as lonely in the original tale, and his wen is simply a physical deformity. Dazai's wood gatherer, quite tipsy at the time, seems drawn to the demons mainly by their revelry. The demons, in turn, are greatly impressed by the utter spontaneity with which the old man performs his simple folk dance.

Dazai implies that self-dignity and formality are obstacles to friendship and camaraderie. The son of the old man takes his meals in decorous silence and responds in absurdly formal language to the naïve questions of his father. The neighbor exasperates the demons with his self-consciously formal attempt to perform a dance as he declaims a strange poetic passage derived from such diverse sources as Nō drama and Shimazaki Toson. Finally, in a long, emphatic (and totally irrelevant) passage, Dazai intrudes to contemptuously dismiss the reverence accorded by the Japanese to certain paragons of contemporary culture.

The two earlier works already treated in this chapter, *A Retelling of the Tales from the Provinces* and *Tsugaru*, help to illuminate the motives behind Dazai's decision to turn the old man in "Taking the

Wen" into a figure of pathos. In the two earlier works, scenes of warm friendship most commonly occur when men gather together for drinking. In "Taking the Wen" the old man forgets his habitual loneliness and grows ecstatic just once: when he realizes that the creatures before him, although hideous demons, are nonetheless drinkers like himself.

Still, his trust in the demons proves to be misplaced. For, in accordance with the traditional tale, the demons deprive the old man of his sole consolation, the wen he has come to regard as an affectionate grandchild. In the end, a reader might conclude that the demons simply show their true colors. Dazai, however, nullifies such an interpretation with his parting remark. He declares everyone blameless — including the supposedly "envious" neighbor who, by Dazai's correct reading of the original, is guilty only of being overly tense about performing in front of the demons. The tale becomes a comedy of errors demonstrating, in Dazai's terms, the "tragicomedy" of human character. Dazai has returned to the world of "The Monkey's Grave," where the innocent and well-intentioned being becomes victimized by his own actions.

XVIII   *"The Tale of Urashima"*

In "Taking the Wen" Dazai periodically quotes from a children's version of the story passages pertaining to the important events of the plot. In "The Tale of Urashima," on the other hand, he quotes only a snatch or two from a traditional version near the end of his retelling. Indeed, reading Dazai's work, one sometimes has the impression that the author is more intent on elaborating certain of his pet ideas than in rendering a modern version of a traditional tale.

The original Urashima is often referred to as the Japanese Rip Van Winkle. Urashima, a young man from a fishing village, rescues a sea turtle from some mischievous children and sets the animal free on the beach. Later the turtle returns to thank Urashima and to take the young man on his back to the underwater realm of Ryugu. Urashima visits the princess of Ryugu and passes a number of carefree days in her realm before deciding to return home. Upon his departure the princess gives Urashima a small box with instructions never to open it.

When he reaches the beach near his village, Urashima fails to recognize the scenes and people he knew before. Disappointed, he opens the box, in spite of the princess's warning. Thereupon, a puff of white smoke comes forth from the box and Urashima instantly turns into an old man in tatters.

Dazai, assuming a knowledge of the traditional tale in his reader, spends his early paragraphs developing a portrait of Urashima. Dazai's Urashima is an eldest son, with certain pretentions that draw criticism from his younger brother and sister. Proud of his aesthetic and cultural sense, he longs for a world where people are not subjected to the harsh criticisms of others. In this wish, he conceivably represents his creator, Dazai. In most of his attitudes, Urashima resembles the typical eldest son of a propertied family of the times, a conservative in line to inherit the wealth and status that assure a life of comfort.

Thus, his reluctance at first to accept the turtle's offer of a ride is quite understandable. A true aesthete by nature, Urashima believes that such mythical places as Ryugu exist only in the minds of poets. Only after the turtle affirms that criticism and cavil do not exist in the underworld realm and that Urashima's reluctance to make the trip reveals a lack of trust in the turtle does the young man consent to the ride.

When Urashima arrives at the underwater realm, he finds practiced certain ideals he would like to see in human society. For example, the princess who welcomes Urashima possesses a self-reliant composure; she neither criticizes others nor covets their praise for herself. She plays the *koto* or Japanese harp beautifully, with no concern whether others hear her music.

Yet, Urashima soon discovers the negative side of his ideals. After meeting the lovely princess, Urashima follows her toward what he assumes will be her palace. But the human courtesies, along with the bickering, do not exist under the sea. The princess, the turtle explains to Urashima, has already forgotten her guest, as she goes in pursuit of whatever pleases her fancy at the moment.

The underwater world, then, is peaceful (an intimation, perhaps, of Dazai's suicide by drowning); but it is not very interesting. There is no anxiety and, thus, in Dazai's terms, there can be no literature. Urashima spends his days eating, drinking cherry wine, and, eventually, frolicking in the princess's chamber. But, as he finally admits, he "is a human and belongs on land." Again, unlike the turtle ("Is this amphibious creature a fish of the sea or a reptile of the land?" Urashima ponders), he is all of a piece and cannot divide his time between two fundamentally different spheres. Ultimately, Urashima turns missionary. Unwilling to simply renounce the peace of the underwater world for the interest of the human, he decides to teach this latter world the ideals he has learned.

Dazai's narrative from the departure of Urashima for home to the end is much closer to the traditional tale than the early part of his work. Within the narration of events, only one crucial difference occurs: the princess in Dazai's version says nothing in giving the box to Urashima.

The traditional tale, brief and cryptic, does not venture a statement as to the moral of the events. Dazai, however, seems bent on wrenching some significance from these strange happenings. He spends several paragraphs examining the differences between the outcome of the Greek story of "Pandora's Box" and the Urashima legend. Since the gods were taking revenge on man and the box still contained "hope" after all the evils were let loose, the Greek tale seems more acceptable to "human" understanding than the Japanese. Nevertheless, Dazai regards "The Tale of Urashima" as representative of the "profound compassion" discernible in the Japanese fairy tale. "The passing of time is man's salvation; forgetfulness is man's salvation," the author recites in almost the final lines of his work. The nostalgia Urashima might feel for the past is swiftly foreclosed as he moves three hundred years into the future. And, Dazai adds with no warrant from the traditional tale, he "lived ten years thereafter as a happy old man."

XIX   *"The Crackling Mountain"*

More clearly than the other three works of this collection, "The Crackling Mountain" reveals Dazai's method of abstracting a "moral" or "truth" from the original tale, then clarifying his discovery by alterations and additions in the retelling. In Dazai's version of "The Crackling Mountain," the traditionally virtuous hare is revealed as a scheming vixen while the traditionally villainous badger becomes a pathetic victim of cruelty.[26]

In the traditional tale an old man and his wife have a pet hare. One day a badger gobbles up the food intended for the hare. Seizing the badger, the old man ties him to a tree and threatens to kill him. When the man goes off to cut wood, the desperate badger cajoles the wife into setting him free. Then, avenging himself on the old man, the badger kills the wife and makes a broth with her remains. When the old man returns, the badger transforms himself into the form of the wife and serves the dish. After the meal the badger assumes his true form and tells the man he has just relished the remains, not of a badger, but of his wife.

Having learned of the tragedy, the hare determines to wreak vengeance on the badger. First, the hare sets fire to the faggots the badger carries on his back. (The title of the story derives from a remark during this episode; when the badger detects a strange "crackling" sound at his back, the hare explains away the phenomenon as a regular occurrence on "Crackling Mountain.") Later, feigning concern, the hare applies a poultice of cayenne pepper to the badger's back. The climax occurs as the hare tricks the badger into making a journey to the moon in a clay boat. The hare ventures forth on a river in his wood boat, followed by the badger in his boat of clay. Only when the badger's boat begins to sink does the hare show his true feelings. In the vivid language of Mitford's translation:

. . . then the hare, seizing his paddle and brandishing it in the air, struck savagely at the badger's boat until he had smashed it to pieces, and killed his enemy.
When the old man heard that his wife's death had been avenged, he was glad in his heart, and more than ever petted the hare, whose brave deeds had caused him to welcome the returning spring.[27]

From the opening paragraph of his retelling, Dazai evinces a concern for the fate of the badger. Apparently the children's version Dazai read to his daughter had the badger wound rather than kill the old woman. His daughter, reacting to the violence of the conclusion, remarked about the "poor badger," and Dazai seems to have sympathized with her response. Upset in particular with what he regarded as the unjust treatment of the badger, Dazai decided to give both animals in the tale entirely new representational roles.

The hare becomes an attractive girl of sixteen, with a dawning realization of her power over infatuated males. The badger becomes a thirty-seven-year-old man, a lecher and glutton with an extremely dark complexion. It should be added that Dazai does not portray these two figures as a girl and a man; he merely says that, in fact, the badger is such a man and the hare such a girl. Focusing intently on these two figures, Dazai, except for brief references, eliminates the old man and woman from his account.

As with the two previous tales, Dazai adds "personalities" to the cardboard figures of the traditional badger and hare. The badger, anxious to present himself in the best possible light to the hare, lies about his age and shows himself willing to go along with the merest whim of the hare. But so lazy and lecherous is the badger that he cannot conceal these weaknesses and thus becomes an easy prey for the watchful hare.

To a degree Dazai describes the badger in terms suggestive of himself. The dark complexion of the animal recalls an adolescent concern of the author; the actual age of the badger is perilously close to Dazai's at the time he wrote the tale. When the badger drools in sexual anticipation, packs a lunch in a box the size of an "oil can," or fails to see that the hare selling him medicine is the vengeful hare, the reader is sorely tempted to conclude that Dazai's penchant for self-satire is again at work. And then, one reads in the commentary by Okuno Tateo that Dazai in fact is poking fun at a friend, Tanaka Eiko. With that piece of knowledge, there dawns a new realization concerning Dazai's art: he has developed methods of comedy and satire so firmly in his earlier works of self-denigration that the attempt to satirize another runs the risk of emerging as self-satire. Dazai had saddled himself with a method, and he remained in large measure subject to the limitations of that method until the final work of his career, a brief fragment entitled "Good-bye."

XX *"The Split-Tongue Sparrow"*

Like two other stories in the volume, "The Split-Tongue Sparrow" describes an adventure involving an elderly married couple. As in the case of "Taking the Wen," the couple in "The Split-Tongue Sparrow" are at odds with one another.

The old man has a pet sparrow which he nurtures with great care. One day the sparrow pecks away at his wife's starch paste, whereupon the enraged woman cuts out the sparrow's tongue. When the old man returns and hears that the unfortunate sparrow has fled, he decides to search out the bird.

Presently the old man finds himself at the sparrow's home in the woods. After a hospitable reception and visit with the sparrow's family, the old man is offered the choice of a parting gift. Two wicker baskets, one heavy and one light, are put before him. Explaining that he is too decrepit to carry a heavy burden, the old man chooses the lighter basket and sets out for home. When he opens the basket at home, he discovers a treasure of gold, silver, and other valuables.

His wife, unable to control her greed, asks the way to the sparrow's home and immediately sets out in hopes of securing a second treasure. She manages to find the house and persuade the sparrow to offer her a gift. Once again, two wicker baskets are brought forth, and the woman unhesitatingly chooses the heavier one. On the way home she opens her booty — only to release a host of goblins who torment and frighten her to death. The old man adopts a son and lives a prosperous life thenceforth.

In his recreation of "The Split-Tongue Sparrow," Dazai again acts more as commentator than storyteller. He explains that he initially intended to include among his stories the celebrated tale of "Peach-Boy." However, Peach-Boy is simply too perfect a hero for Dazai's taste. A weak person like himself, Dazai apologizes, simply cannot identify with such a hero.

Of course, self-abasement is a theme common to much of Dazai's writing. But, as Edward Seidensticker has pointed out, Dazai's self-abasement alternates with sudden manifestations of pride. In his version of "The Split-Tongue Sparrow" there is no such explicit manifestation by the author. Yet, in remarking that the old man is not quite forty years old, Dazai hints that the man is a surrogate for himself and thus nudges the reader to identify the old man's psychology as his own.

The old man makes an interesting study. A subdued, gentle creature almost overwhelmed by a shrewish wife, the old man can scarcely articulate his ideas and reactions. He feels most comfortable bent over a book or scattering seeds for his pet sparrow. Only in conversing with the sparrow does the old man show himself verbally adept. Late in Dazai's story, when he finds the sparrow mute because of her split tongue, the old man is perfectly content, as the sparrow also seems to be, to sit and enjoy the quiet.

Such a man can hardly endure the assaults of criticism. When his wife claims she overheard him talking in their house to a girl with a charming voice and demands an explanation, the old man meekly acknowledges his conversation with the sparrow. Imagine a callous wife accepting a tale like that! And, even when the sparrow criticizes him for inactivity, the old man can only claim that he is hopefully awaiting the arrival of a task he alone can perform.

How seriously should the reader take this old man? Dazai's ending, though slightly different from the traditional version, has the old man surviving his greedy wife to live in prosperity. The old man in Dazai's tale attains a high official position, and refers sardonically to the role his wife's "efforts" have played in his rise to prominence.

Dazai does not explicitly show any sympathy for the pathetic wife. Yet, recalling his sympathetic treatment of the traditionally evil badger of "The Crackling Mountain" and the envious old neighbor of "Taking the Wen," one wonders whether the author didn't harbor like sympathy for the woman. Shrewish and greedy she is. But she does hear her husband speaking to someone with a charming, feminine voice; and she is unable to communicate with him, not because he is genuinely timid, but simply because pride keeps him from dealing with people in a normal, human way. Perhaps the old man is correct in claiming that people simply lie to one another and, therefore, it is best to remain silent. But the reader of Dazai suspects that his author was capable of regarding such an attitude as a mere pretention of superiority, as he hinted in "Mount Yoshino." Again, in portraying the sparrow as a puppet two feet high, Dazai, according to Okuno Tateo, intimates that the old man's interest in his pet is erotic in nature. There is little in the man's reactions to the sparrow to confirm such a judgment, but one is always left with the unsolved question of why Dazai changed the neutral, colorless sparrow of the traditional work into a young female with an enchanting voice.

XXI *Dazai as Moralist*

A study of Japanese sources on Dazai's life yields little detailed information on the author's activities during these war years. No doubt the limitations on Japanese life imposed by the government and by the necessities of the war itself prevented Dazai from fully indulging himself in his habitual activities. And lacking recent experience in attempted suicide and drug addiction, he wrote nothing significant on his own initiative in his customary "autobiographical" manner. The critic of Dazai is strongly tempted to see in this negative evidence for the proposition that the autobiographical subject most appealing to Dazai was himself in extreme difficulty.

Unable perhaps to make himself such an interesting subject during the war, Dazai turned by and large for his writing inspiration to the sources already dealt with in this chapter. Though he used such sources, Dazai remained himself; the style of the works is one in which only Dazai could have written. In examining these works, the student of Dazai constantly discovers expressions and gestures characteristic of the author.

The works of this period differ from the early, more autobiographical pieces in their relatively more precise moral commentary. Given, for example, a samurai from Saikaku or a badger and a hare from a Japanese fairy tale, Dazai's sense of irony usually went to work trying to find the real (as opposed to the traditional) moral quality of these actors. The reader senses even in the animal legends the same quality of ironic distance between author and character as he found between the author and his Dazai-like protagonists in the early works.

CHAPTER 5

The Postwar Years (1946-1948)

I *The Biography*

AFTER the war Dazai remained with his family at Kanagi until November, 1946. Perhaps the death of his grandmother in October had some connection with Dazai's departure, for he now found himself alone among his more or less hostile brothers. The pleasure he had experienced in coming to terms in recent years with the elder members of the family probably dissipated with the loss of his grandmother, the last of his surviving ancestors.

In the aftermath of the war Dazai was, for a Japanese of that period, remarkably sanguine. His optimism found at least a guarded expression in the very title he chose for his principal book during his postwar stay in Kanagi, *Pandora's Box*. In that work Dazai wrote:

Human beings are incapable of despair. They may often be deceived in their hopes, but they are also deceived in their despairs. Let's put the matter straight. Even as a person stumbles and rolls around in the depths of sorrow, he reaches at some moment for a thread of hope.[1]

Another likely factor in Dazai's return to Tokyo was the desire to oppose the opportunists who were joining the bandwagon of "democracy." With the American occupation forces intent on purging militaristic imperialism from Japanese society, people who a few years back had worshiped the emperor now came forward as dyed-in-the-wool democrats. Dazai, who had held himself aloof from the war fervor, observed the contradiction with his inherent sense of irony. Now he came forward to challenge, not so much that friend of his youth, democracy, as the selfishness of the people and the superficiality of their convictions. "Tenno Heika! Banzai! — Long live the Emperor!" Dazai exulted in one of his first postwar pieces.[2]

This development clearly reveals the rationale which, perhaps more than any other, determined Dazai's moral posture at any given time. Wary of committing himself to any doctrinaire position, he lies in wait for someone else to make a foolish move. And even when he lashes out at the "enemy," he is constantly — and ironically — aware of the partial and relative nature of his own standpoint.

Returning to his old home in Mitaka City in Tokyo under these circumstances, Dazai was unable, perhaps unwilling, to recapture the contentment of the first five or six years of his married life. The short story "The Father," published in April, 1947, describes better than any other source Dazai's rejection of his responsibilities as a husband and father. With two children and a devoted, pregnant wife, Dazai could not find within himself the wherewithal to sustain his family. Although he could no longer appeal to the family in Kanagi for aid, he had now attained sufficient stature as a writer to ensure a steady demand for articles and stories. He had conquered certain problems which had nagged him in the past. He no longer took drugs; he no longer contracted debts.

Still, as such additional works as "Cherries," "Villon's Wife," and parts of *No Longer Human* show, Dazai could not become one with his family. Recognizing his obligation to support and guide his wife and children, regretting every lapse which deprived them of that support and guidance, Dazai nevertheless grew more and more irresponsible. Almost every night found him in a *nomiya* (a small cozy bar) or at an *odenya* (a bar specializing in *oden*, or Japanese hotchpotch), frittering away the money that should have gone into doctor bills and medicine for his wife and clothing for his children. Although Dazai at times claimed his manner of life was a protest against the times, the stories which sprang from his experience suggest a man in the grip of some uncontrollable fate. The Dazai-father figure of the stories takes resolutions to mend his ways, but some unexpected turn of events usually catches him off guard and plunges him once again into dissipation.

Dazai took his postwar dissipation in both women and drink. In the early days of the war he had had an affair with a young woman named Ota Shizuko. In February, 1947, Dazai decided to resume the liaison. He spent a week at Shizuko's house in Shimosoga in Kanagawa Prefecture, then moved on to the house of an old friend, Tanaka Eiko, in Ise. Next he moved to a nearby inn and, finally, early in March, to a rented room near his home in Mitaka. During this period Dazai was again writing at a furious pace. And, as was his custom, he stayed away from home — to avoid distractions, no doubt, but also perhaps to avoid the "counterpull" of an environment at odds with the subject and tone of the work he was writing.

Shizuko, Dazai's friend, had long hoped to become a writer. But, for some reason, she had given up. She turned instead to Dazai: "Since I could no longer write, I gave my diary to him, and asked him to write something from that. Not only my diary. I gave him my soul and my body. I wanted to lose myself and let something come to flower within him. I felt I would be content to die, once I saw myself in him."[3]

Dazai must have seen the possibilities in Shizuko's diary. By the end of July, four months after he began writing, he had finished *The Setting Sun*, a novel which in Donald Keene's translation seems to have created more interest in Dazai in this country than any other of the author's translated works.

Shizuko soon presented Dazai with something more than a diary. In November she gave birth to a girl to be named Haruko. Thus, in real life, Dazai played for Shizuko the role the novelist Uehara plays for Kazuko in *The Setting Sun*. Dazai, we might say, had the opportunity in *The Setting Sun* of depending at the same time on his two favorite story sources: a "history" already written (as in *A Retelling of the Tales from the Provinces*) and his own experience (as in all the autobiographical works).

Shizuko's daughter Haruko was Dazai's fourth child. His wife Michiko had already given birth to the author's third child, a girl, shortly after Dazai returned from his sojourn with Shizuko in Kanagawa Prefecture. The reader of *The Setting Sun*, forewarned, is tempted to see in the gentle submissiveness of Uehara's wife a quality that Dazai evidently found in Michiko.

Dazai was a genius at making a bad situation worse. In March, having left Shizuko pregnant in Kanagawa and returned to his own pregnant wife in Mitaka, Dazai found a new companion at the local noodle shop. Yamazaki Tomie was a young war widow who supported herself by working in a beauty parlor. With more reason for despondency than Dazai, Tomie proved an ideal companion in dissipation. She would drink with him, take down the stories he dictated, and — above all — lend a sympathetic ear to his talk of despair and death.

"Shuji, you seem so distraught every day. Do you feel as though you're always shuddering?"

"Yes, I think I want to die."

"Let's go on as far as we can. And kill ourselves when we have the chance. Okay?"[4]

This conversation was recorded in Yamazaki Tomie's diary for January 11, 1948. She had not yet known Dazai for a year.

During the period of his affair with Yamazaki Tomie, Dazai wrote what many Japanese critics and readers consider his greatest work, *No Longer Human*. Dazai relied on many of his own experiences in writing the work, but rearranged and sharpened the episodes far beyond his usual degree in the autobiographical works.[5] Once *No Longer Human* began to appear serially in the *Asahi News* from May 15, 1948, Dazai set to work on his next piece. His title: "Good-bye."

Dazai never finished "Good-bye." Together with Yamazaki Tomie, he dropped out of sight on June 13, 1948. Several notes he left behind, including one to his wife complaining he could no longer write and simply wished to go to some "unknown land," suggested that Dazai was again bent on suicide. Even his more sanguine friends felt little hope this time. In a moving essay, written a day or two following the news of Dazai's disappearance, Kamei Katsuichiro wrote of Dazai's once telling him how he would like to fake a suicide. Once he had been presumed dead, his acquaintances would feel free to express their true feelings and opinions about him. Then, Dazai added, he would reappear — to discover who his true friends were and to embarrass the "false friends" who had betrayed him.[6]

But, Kamei felt, Dazai would not come back this time. And he was right. On June 19, the bodies of Dazai and Yamazaki Tomie were dredged from the Tamagawa Watercourse, approximately one thousand yards downstream from where, it was surmised, they had leapt in. If Dazai had lived he would have celebrated his thirty-ninth birthday that very day.

II   "A Yearbook of Agonies"

"A Yearbook of Agonies," a kind of autobiography describing certain crucial stages in Dazai's life, appeared in 1946 in the March issue of *New Literature*. Disgusted by the postwar opportunism of many Japanese, Dazai discussed his "intellectual development" to show the unreliability — for one Japanese, at least — of ideology and all its trappings.

Dazai's method is disarming. He begins by referring to the democratic tendencies of his youth in such earlier works as "Remembrances." The reader hears again the story of the baby Dazai's remark about the Emperor Meiji and the "Living God," of the boy

Dazai's bewilderment over why his mother blamed democracy for rising taxes, of the student Dazai's argument with a teacher over the question of the equality between student and teacher, between child and parent. Later the author describes, more suggestively if not in more detail than in other works, his activities as a Communist sympathizer during his university days. With a relatively comfortable allowance he gave the poor Communist students food, clothes, shoes, and, on occasion, even money. He once mentions trying his hand at proletarian literature, but coyly refrains from recording his pseudonym or any details of what he wrote. But Dazai refuses to regard the postwar "new liberalism" as even a partial victory for the Communists. With Socialists and Communists out of jail and organizing their cause, with the conservatives and militarists banned from public life, Dazai stayed aloof from politics. Suddenly he found a hitherto hidden affection for the emperor, inspired to a great extent by anger toward those who formerly revered but now attacked the emperor.

Apparently, Dazai was by nature attracted to the cause of the underdog. For those who would charge him with inconsistency, he offers a telling reply: "For me there is no such thing as thought. Either I like something or I hate it."[7] Perhaps this is only anti-ideology, perhaps thoroughgoing anti-intellectualism. At the very least, Dazai's attitude arose partly in response to the fickle way many Japanese of the time switched their ideological allegiance.

Dazai, as one might suspect, does not mind a person changing his mind or even contradicting himself in the next breath. He had himself completely reversed his position — at least on one level. (As Dazai was well aware, there was, on another level, a consistency in his belief that one could be free only in standing apart from the crowd.) He pours scorn on the so-called thinkers because, in looking over his own life, he can recall believing certain things at various moments but no process of reasoning which brought him to belief at those moments. To realize what a facile thing reasoning is, listen, he advises his readers, to the contemporary ideologue explaining his dramatic conversion.

Despite his disgust with present conditions, Dazai harbors vague, utopian hopes for Japan's future. The postwar liberalism, like the mood of the 1920's, is a shallow thing; somehow, though, Dazai feels the current mood will give rise to something permanent and good. Near the end of "A Yearbook of Agonies," Dazai warms to this possibility. If they face the future bravely and submit to the moral guidance of the emperor, the Japanese can make a "paradise" of their country.

Dazai, however, is not very convincing in his role as a visionary. Indeed, except insofar as they influenced Dazai's own behavior and writing objectives, his thoughts on postwar Japan seem hardly worth considering.

Previously Dazai had often written for the sake of what he termed "service." More pertinently, he had participated in the Communist movement — partly, at least — to "serve" a cause destined to fail. In "A Yearbook of Agonies" the notion of "service" is transformed into one of pure "self-sacrifice." Dazai praises the idea of "unrewarded action" and "unselfish activity." Attracted to the figure of the suffering Christ, Dazai probably gained this notion partly from reading the New Testament.

Dazai habitually enjoyed thinking of himself in the company of the great, including Christ. In thinking of self-sacrifice he was, of course, thinking of himself. Only a few paragraphs before his explanation of self-sacrifice, he had written that there was "nothing left for him other than death."[8] One central question will plague the reader of Dazai at this point. Was Dazai, once again in a suicide mood, looking for an idea to give his contemplated death some meaning (or status!), or did the desire to destroy his life grow naturally from what he regarded as a command from history?

III   *"The Fifteen Year Era"*

"The Fifteen Year Era," published in the April issue of *Cultural View*, modifies some of the impressions created by "A Yearbook of Agonies," published one month earlier. When considering his life concretely, Dazai could not put himself in an utterly "pure" frame of mind. He admits a degree of concern about the reaction of his readers. "Let them say," he writes apropos of his wartime works, "that at least I opposed the hypocrisy of the salon school of writing."[9]

On the other hand, some of Dazai's words in "The Fifteen Year Era" give additional meaning and depth to certain vague pronouncements in "A Yearbook of Agonies." His negative notion of freedom, implicit in the reversal of his feelings about the emperor, is clarified in a parable. A pigeon, it seems, was once so anxious to fly faster that he asked God to remove the air which seemed to be slowing his progress. Of course he quickly discovered that, without the air, he could not fly at all. Likewise, Dazai points out, the free man needs opposition; he cannot express his feelings in a vacuum.

Again, his premonition that he will soon die because he has no other option acquires credibility as Dazai explains why he didn't commit suicide during the war. He admits to no great concern for the welfare of his wife and children — a curious posture in view of his expressed worry that his death in war would cause his family great hardship. Rather, in a sentence reminiscent of his hesitation over describing too closely the coastal scenery in *Tsugaru*, he says he could not commit suicide because this would only encourage the enemy and demoralize those friends of the author in the armed forces.

Furthermore, Dazai partially clarifies his feelings about the future course of events in Japan. More accurately, perhaps, he tells why he feels Japan might transform itself into a paradise. His own generation has lost its chance. Among his old friends some lost out by being expelled from school; others were thrown into jail; and still others died in the war or committed suicide. In describing the lost hopes of his pathetic generation, Dazai is on the trail of one of his large themes in *The Setting Sun*. His generation has failed and should clear out to make way for the young, even for the unborn.

Perhaps Dazai's hope for the young generation sprang from the memories of his own youth, which undoubtedly flooded his mind when he fled from Tokyo to Tsugaru in the final year of the war. At the very beginning of "The Fifteen Year Era" he confesses that his return to Tsugaru has shown him that he is "a farmer after all."[10] He must write about his life once again because what he wrote five years ago as a city resident in "Eight Views of Tokyo" has, in his more recent experience, proved inadequate. His reconciliation with the elder members of his family and with his past — indeed, to the simple life of the farms and villages so movingly described in *Tsugaru* — gives rise in "The Fifteen Year Era" to disgust with the sophisticated influences of the city. Dazai describes his endless changes of residence in Tokyo; he decries the salon school of writing and the pressure to conform. At one point, Dazai declares that he has come to appreciate Tsugaru for the first time only during his protracted stay at the end of the war. Then he goes into raptures almost immediately over the possible birth of a "new culture" which will nourish a "new expression of love."[11] Although Dazai himself does not make the connection, his insistence on valuing the simple over the sophisticated and the ugly over the beautiful must have arisen in part from his recognition of how superior Tsugaru — his home — was to Tokyo — his nemesis.

IV *"Villon's Wife"*

The reader of Dazai's postwar fiction cannot but be struck by the number of first-person female narrators. Three of his best works — "Villon's Wife," "Osan," and *The Setting Sun* — are narrated in the first person by the leading female character. "Villon's Wife" and "Osan" are, in addition, narrated by a woman burdened with one or more children and married to a drunken sot who shows little concern for providing them with the necessities of life. Another postwar story, "Cherries," again has as the main female character a long-suffering wife of the same stamp. In this instance, though, the drunken husband-writer narrates the story. Dazai, one might suppose, had generously allowed Michiko a hearing with his readers and would not deny himself the same chance.

"Villon's Wife" was published in 1947 in the March issue of the periodical *Cultural View*. Highly praised at the time of publication for its evocation of the *après guerre* mood of despair and frivolity, "Villon's Wife" has, with the passage of time, lost some of its attraction for Japanese critics.[12] Regardless of this, most critics still rank it, along with *The Setting Sun* and *No Longer Human*, among Dazai's finest postwar pieces.[13]

The first scene in "Villon's Wife" takes place at night in the home of a well-known writer. His wife, sleeping along with their four-year-old son, hears someone open the front door, then rummage around in drawers. As she suspects, it is her husband, returning home from one of his customary drinking sprees. Tonight, though, the situation proves more serious than usual. Shortly after the husband's return, a middle-aged man and wife begin pounding on the front door. The husband, it turns out, has just taken a considerable amount of money from the bar they run. He denies the accusation. But when he pulls a knife on his accuser, then flees into the street, the wife realizes the truth of their accusation. Obviously, her husband, aware that he was being followed, had rummaged about in the drawers a few moments before in search of the knife.

Having promised to compensate for the theft, the wife goes the following day to the bar of the middle-aged couple. There she promises to work as a waitress until the debt is cleared. To show her sincerity she starts work immediately, even though she has brought her son.

Eventually her husband sees to it that the stolen sum is returned. But his wife, attracted by the coarseness and jocularity of the

customers and anxious to clear the drinking debt, decides to stay on
at the bar. The husband, who occasionally shows up with another
woman, seems himself satisfied with the arrangement. The story
ends with the wife, having been virtually raped by a customer at her
home, making plans to live permanently at the bar.

"Villon's Wife" tends to defy attempts to articulate its structure
and themes. In certain parts of the work Dazai appears to confront
the grim character of life in postwar Japan in ways that far transcend
the usual sociological tags; in other parts of the work he has the husband spout about God and death in a manner that seems only
pseudo-mysterious.

Cearly, though, Dazai wrote "Villon's Wife" in a mood of deep
seriousness. Laughter, an important motif in the story, is unrelated
to humor or comedy. Rather, events become so intractable that
laughter is the only response possible.

Despite their ill luck and the bleak nature of their lives, the
characters in "Villon's Wife" have enough goodwill and pluck to
assure their survival. Whether they have merely small ambitions or
none at all, they seem ready to make the adjustments in their lives
that circumstances demand. For example, events of significance occur to the wife, but (except momentarily for the robbery and the
chase) she does not see them as important. The times have made her
so numb that a rape seems no more significant than buying a bun.

Despite its literary quality, the story's high reputation in Japan
rests in part on its impact at the time of publication. Just emerging
from the ravages of the war, the Japanese were doubtless moved by
the concluding words, the most powerful of the entire story. After
her husband has claimed he stole the money to buy New Year's
presents and argued that this proves he is "not a monster," his wife
retorts: "His words didn't make me especially glad. I said, 'There's
nothing wrong with being a monster, is there? As long as we can stay
alive.' "[14]

V *"The Father"*

The student of Dazai, however, gains his best appreciation of
"Villon's Wife" only in considering it in conjunction with three
other stories from the postwar period: "The Father," "Cherries,"
and "Osan." "The Father" seems to be fairly straightforward
autobiography. Published in the periodical *Human* in February,
1947, the story presents, together with "Cherries," the point of view
of the father. That father, a reflection of Dazai, does not appear very

attractive. He squanders his money on drink while his wife and children go without proper food and clothing. One day his wife asks him to stay home and watch the children while she goes to pick up their portion of rationed rice. Aware that she has a severe cold, the father agrees. Yet, when the lady from a nearby *oden* shop comes to announce that a woman is waiting for him, the father deserts the children. The story ends with the father, in the company of the woman, on his way for a round of drinks with several friends. Inadvertently he passes near the line of people waiting to receive the rationed rice. When his wife and older child notice him, the wife merely pretends she has not seen him while trying to distract the child's attention.

Dazai has little to say in his own defense. Although he had found married life congenial before and during the war, he now declares: "The happiness of the hearth — why am I incapable of achieving that? I can't even endure being around it. There's something frightening about a hearth."[15] Finally, in the last sentence of "The Father," the father-Dazai figure admits he is simply a weak person. The tendency to submit to fate, so strong in the pre - *Final Years* period, was again coming to the fore.

VI *"Cherries"*

"Cherries" once again gives the father's viewpoint. Published in the journal *The World* in May, 1947, "Cherries" reflects what might be termed its author's "numbness." Okuno Tateo finds "Cherries" so closely connected with Dazai's imminent suicide that he describes it as a "last will and literary testament."

The "I" who narrates "Cherries" often refers to himself as "father," and to the other persons in the account as "mother" and "children." Although the narrative as a consequence has an abstract quality about it, the reader attuned to Dazai finds, as usual, allusions that imply further details. The father, of course, is Dazai. The mother appears to be a stronger-willed person than the submissive wife (the real Michiko?) of "The Father." Okuno Tateo describes "Cherries" as, in one sense, a "work of marital quarreling," and Dazai himself admits at one point in the narrative to being always on the losing end of the argument. Finally, the four-year-old son of "Cherries" seems transferred almost straight from "Villon's Wife." In the latter work, the son is also four, but "actually smaller than most two-year-olds. He is not even sure on his feet, and as for talking, it's all he can do to say 'yum-yum' or 'ugh.' Sometimes I wonder if he is not feebleminded."[16] In "Cherries" the boy remains skinny, barely able to stand and speak. For good measure, he refuses to be toilet trained.

In "Cherries," Dazai confesses that he has no talent for handling the problems and tasks of everyday living. At times, the reader may suspect the author is proud, not ashamed, of this fact. At one point he declares: "It is not that I can't learn about rationing, registration, and such matters. I simply have no time to learn."[17] Many readers will regard this as Dazai's expression of contempt toward a part of life he could not master. One should not, however, dismiss the possibility that Dazai, at such moments, conceivably sensed the imminence of his own death.

"Cherries" ends with the narrator ensconced in a *nomiya* intending to drink away the evening. He has just come from home after quarreling with his wife. When the proprietor of the *nomiya* brings him some cherries, the narrator reflects:

I never give my children at home any costly food. Probably they've never seen cherries in their entire lives. If I gave them some they'd probably be overjoyed. They would be overjoyed if I took some home.

If they string them on a thread, these cherries would probably make a pretty coral necklace.

But the father eats one of the cherries piled on the plate. Bites as though the fruit were sour, then spits out the seed. Eats another and spits out the seed. Eats another and spits out the seed, murmuring to himself as though he were threatening someone: "The parent is more precious than the child."[18]

VII "*Osan*"

"Osan" (the title comes from the name of the wife-heroine in the story) was suggested in part by Chikamatsu Monzaemon's *The Love Suicides of Amijima*.[19] In the Chikamatsu play Osan is married to Jihei, a paper merchant. Jihei has fallen in love with the geisha Koharu, to the neglect of his family and his business.

Early in the play Koharu receives a letter from Osan begging her to renounce Jihei.[20] Koharu, moved by Osan's appeal, behaves so rudely as to turn Jihei against her, provoking him at one point to kick her in the face. Later Osan comes to regret her letter. Though he has officially broken with Koharu, Jihei cannot forget her. Furthermore, his rival for Koharu is on the verge of ransoming her, a great setback for Jihei's reputation as a businessman. Osan, aware of Koharu's great nobility, urges Jihei to himself rescue Koharu, "if only for the sake of his reputation as a merchant." As the title indicates, Jihei and Koharu eventually commit suicide.

Dazai turned Chikomatsu's play into a sketch reflecting his own experience as a husband and father, premonitions about his fate, and the implicit similarities between his domestic problems and those of Jihei the paper merchant. Osan, the narrator of Dazai's story, notices her husband slipping out of the house one evening. Until his return at noon the following day, Osan passes a considerable time reviewing the course of their marriage. During their ten years together, neither spouse has felt much affection for the other. She realizes that her husband has, until lately, fulfilled his role as adequately as most Japanese husbands in an arranged marriage. He has worked steadily at a publishing firm and, on occasion, even helped Osan tend her small garden. Only once has he been truly angry with her, and he has never beaten her.

Matters have taken a turn for the worse from the moment the American planes partially destroyed their house in a western suburb of Tokyo. While Osan returned home to Aomori with the children, her husband stayed behind in the one remaining room of the house, commuting each day for work to downtown Tokyo. When Osan returned several months later, she found her husband uncertain and timid. The publishing firm had collapsed and the attempt to start a new publishing venture had failed. Her husband was keeping regular company with other women.

When her husband returns from his night out, Osan seems the patient, understanding wife. Far from reproaching him, she makes him at home, serving him the beer she has kept on ice since the previous day. The 'husband, as reflected in Osan's account, seems a gentle man. He is affectionate toward his children and even turns lachrymose as he hears a neighbor's radio broadcasting the French national anthem.

Their life together continues uneventful through the warmest days of the summer; then the husband abruptly declares that he is leaving for a hot spring resort. Osan helps him prepare for his journey and the next day sees him off at the front door. Three days later she learns from a newspaper that her husband has drowned himself along with his mistress. Shortly thereafter, she receives a letter written by her husband just before the suicide which purports to explain his motives.

Most of Dazai's implied parallels with Chikamatsu's *The Love Suicides at Amijima* occur in the last part of his story and seem at least partly ironic. He makes his most subtle, effective parallel in the scene where the husband, about to set out for the hot spring, asks his wife to put his traveling clothes in order. In the play Osan's father finds his daughter's clothes missing from the bureau drawer when he comes at Jihei's prompting to take her back to his home; in Dazai's story a similar scene occurs when Osan herself cannot locate her husband's clothes. The difference within the parallel reveals a difference between the two Osans. Chikamatsu's heroine had urged Jihei to sell her clothes for Koharu's ransom. Dazai's Osan never shows such imaginative sympathy.

Like Jihei, the husband in Dazai's story commits suicide with his mistress. Their suicide, however, is hardly in the romantic tradition governing the *"michiyuki"*[21] and the suicide of so many Chikamatsu lovers. In a farewell letter to his Osan, Dazai's husband declares that love is not involved; he has simply determined to "mount the cross of the revolutionary. . . . If my death contributes even in a small way to making our contemporary demons ponder their own shame, I'll be happy."[22] To the wife this is mere rhetoric. The facts of the autopsy alone reveal her husband's motive: his mistress was pregnant.

That Dazai was concerned in the series of stories from "Villon's Wife" to "Osan" with problems facing him in life and with the responses a wife might give to behavior such as his seems scarcely arguable. "The Father" and "Cherries" are more like vignettes than genuine short stories. They seem closest to the facts of Dazai's life, a scarcely surprising observation in view of the fact that these two stories represent the father's point of view. "Villon's Wife" and "Osan" are more literary; indeed, their very titles suggest the author was searching beyond his experience for the resources to tell his story.

Dazai then had to rely on his imaginative understanding to portray the wife's point of view in all four tales. Perhaps as a consequence, the wives are better drawn; they are more lively and interesting as characters. The reader knows the father will yield to the temptation which, sooner or later, will inevitably present itself. The wife, on the other hand, seems free to submit, to fight back, or to go her own way. Dazai knew himself; he knew his own weaknesses. Presumably he knew his wife, her reactions and feelings. Yet, in "Villon's Wife" and "Osan" at least, he seems more interested in how a wife might react to a scoundrel like himself, rather than in how Michiko did react.

An interesting though oversimple scheme suggests itself in these stories. "The Father" and "Cherries" are closest to reality, giving Dazai's sense of his own weakness and timid excuses for his irresponsible behavior. The father figure in each story seems hemmed in by family life and obligations. He tries to escape by leaving the house to drink and seek the company of women, but he finds no pleasure in dissipation. Unable to renounce his wife and children, he drifts into self-pity and pseudo-religious yearning, muttering about the "preciousness" of fathers and quoting the beginning of Psalm 121: I will lift up mine eyes unto the hills. In "Osan" Dazai shows a more characteristic side, humor and curiosity in the midst of adversity. He wrote this story conscious of certain distasteful thoughts: that he had fathered an illegitimate child, was carrying on an affair with a second dangerous woman, and was probably heading for suicide. Did Michiko know? If she did, what did she think? Would she view his weakness with the same indulgence as the victim?

Dazai, of course, was not so melodramatic. Knowing his sense of irony, the reader wonders whether Dazai himself did not perhaps take the same attitude as, for example, Osan. In short, perhaps Dazai's pleas were mere rhetoric, and he was himself aware of this.

"Villon's Wife" completes the scheme. Perhaps Dazai felt that a wife capable of living a life as promiscuous as his own would be a perfect match. Certainly it would relieve him of certain guilt feelings. If the husband wishes to vulgarize himself, let the wife follow suit. Then the problem might tend to solve itself.

VIII "Family Happiness"

Certain of Dazai's postwar stories do not fit at all into this scheme. One such story, "Family Happiness," does, however, deal with an area of life common to these works. In The Complete Works of Dazai Osamu this piece comes immediately before the final story of that particular series, "Cherries." However, "Family Happiness" was first published only after the author's death, in the July, 1948, issue of The Central Review.

The first part of the story is amusing, but not relevant here. Dazai introduces the reader in random fashion to the elements that make up the tale: the "people," the bureaucracy, and a family radio. The reader soon recognizes Dazai in the "I" of the narrative. As in "The Father" and "Cherries" the father likes to treat himself to food and drink outside the home, but begrudges his family even the smallest expense.

The thread of the story begins with the author listening to an interview program on the radio. A government bureaucrat is talking to the "man in the street." When he finishes, Dazai imagines this bureaucrat going home to be welcomed and flattered by his family. This, says Dazai, is one kind of family happiness; but government bureaucrats can earn it only at the expense of people like himself.

Finally, Dazai asks his reader to imagine another happy family, that of Tsushima Shuji.[23] The name, Dazai adds, does not refer to anyone in particular. If he used another name, that person might take offense.

Tsushima Shuji, government bureaucrat, buys a new radio for his family to replace the one broken three years ago. So anxious is he to return home to show off the radio that he refuses to wait on a lady who has come into the office just at closing time. The lady begs Tsushima to register a birth. When he tells her to come back tomorrow she replies: "If not today, what trouble I'll have tomorrow." That evening the woman drowns herself in the Tamagawa Watercourse. Dazai ends "Family Happiness" with the remark: "Family happiness is the source of every evil."

The story is exceedingly clumsy because Dazai wishes to make a questionable point crystal clear. Possibly Dazai was trying to rationalize his own rejection of "family happiness." No doubt a fine literary work could have grown out of the theme of sacrificing the welfare of outsiders for the selfish purpose of the inner circle of the family. Not even the most sympathetic Dazai reader would claim, however, that the author demonstrated such a theme in "Family Happiness." Indeed, Dazai dismissed the problem much too easily.

As is often the case with Dazai, the reader of "Family Happiness" reaps greater rewards in pondering the implications for the author personally than in analyzing the formal elements of the story. Having begun his narration with a glimpse of what his own home is like, Dazai portrays the model family with an ideal father, ironically named Tsushima Shuji. Dazai carefully delineates in Tsushima a character the precise opposite of himself. Tsushima neither smokes nor drinks. He is up with the dawn each morning looking forward to a day of constructive work. The stingy Dazai of "Family Happiness" berates his wife for buying a radio; the generous Tsushima buys a radio for his family with money won in a lottery. In view of this contrast of character, one is forced to ponder the implications for Dazai Osamu of Tsushima's cruel indifference to the importunate lady. Since Tsushima's concern for the welfare of his family is destructive of society, is one to conclude that Dazai's neglect of his family somehow benefits society?

IX   The Setting Sun

The first of Dazai's two famous postwar novels, *The Setting Sun*
was published initially in serial form. The periodical *New Tide*
carried the work in its issues of July, August, September, and October of 1947. Nine years later Donald Keene translated the work
into English for New Directions. So well did Dazai's novel capture
the spirit of the time that the very word "*Shayozoku*," or "Declining
Aristocracy," became in a short time a popular term.

The Setting Sun is centered on four main characters. Naoji, a
drunk and a dope addict, aspires to become a writer. His older sister
Kazuko is a divorcée living with her mother, the third major
character. Finally, there is the older, established novelist, Uehara,
Kazuko's "lover."

Among these four characters, Kazuko seems most important. She
relates the story of *The Setting Sun* in the first person, and the other
characters appear as actors in her narration. No doubt Kazuko's account of what the others say and do is meant to be trusted; she is too
honest and watchful a person to distort matters by either willfulness
or inadvertence. Furthermore, Naoji gets a chance to speak directly
to the reader when Kazuko discovers his diary, the "Moonflower
Journal."

When the novel opens, Kazuko is living with her mother in Tokyo.
An aristocratic family before the war, they have lost their estate and
their social standing by virtue of the reforms of the American occupation.[24] In the first chapter of the novel they move to a rural cottage in Izu. The mother is sick and weak, but she and her daughter
manage to keep going. They seem quite content, in fact, to live a
diminished but peaceful existence.

Then Naoji, missing in the South Pacific during the war, returns
home. Kazuko regards him as disrupting the peaceful life of her
mother and herself. "Once Naoji returned from the South Pacific,
our real hell began."[25] For the most part, Naoji leads a dissolute life
in Tokyo, returning occasionally to the cottage in Izu to recuperate.
Unlike Kazuko, the mother regards Naoji's behavior with indulgence.

Eventually the mother dies. Afterward Naoji takes his own life,
leaving, in addition to the "Moonflower Journal," a suicide note entitled "Naoji's Testament." He confesses to Kazuko in the testament
that he has felt a genuine love for only one woman — the wife of a
middle-aged artist:

Once I dreamed I held hands with his wife, and I knew at once that she had loved me from long before. . . . I wanted somehow to free myself from his wife's enchantment, to forget it, to have everything over and done with. But it was no use. I am, it would seem, a man who can love only one woman. I can state it quite positively — I have never once felt any of my woman friends was beautiful or lovable except her.[26]

Finally he ends his testament with the simple declaration:

Once more, good-bye
Kazuko.
I am, after all, an aristocrat.[27]

During his testament Naoji once mentions in a hushed tone the name of his love: "Suga."

Her mother and Naoji are gone; only Kazuko remains from the family of aristocrats. Aristocrat in name, Kazuko shows certain peasant qualities. Unlike her feeble mother, Kazuko is robust. She looks back on her period of conscripted labor as her one pleasant experience of the war years. After she and her mother move to Izu, Kazuko readily takes to dressing in peasant garb to dig a vegetable garden.

Kazuko, again unlike her mother, is strong willed. She almost despises her mother for letting her Uncle Wada handle the responsibilities and details of the move to Izu. She finds Naoji's drunken habits despicable. That strong will survives even the change in her attitude toward Naoji, which she experiences near the end of *The Setting Sun*. She discovers, in reading the "Moonflower Journal" and "Naoji's Testament," her brother's genuine worth, his sufferings and sincerity. Then she determines to do something, in part for her dead brother.

Even before Naoji's death Kazuko has set out to make herself dissolute — in a different sense from what, at the time, she considers her brother's degradation. She throws herself at Naoji's mentor, the middle-aged novelist Uehara.

Please see me again and then, if you dislike me, say so plainly. The flames in my breast were lighted by you; it is up to you to extinguish them. I can't put them out by my unaided efforts. If we meet, if we can only meet, I know that I shall be saved. Were these the days of *The Tale of Genji*, what I am saying now would not be anything exceptional, but today — oh my ambition is to become your mistress and the mother of your child.[28]

Kazuko sleeps with Uehara one night; the next morning Naoji commits suicide.

After Naoji's funeral Kazuko, who has now read the testament, writes a final note to Uehara. The chapter containing her note, the last of the novel, is called "Victims." The word reflects both certain portions of Kazuko's note and the fact that Kazuko's mother and Naoji have been sacrificed to the dictates of the time. It also refers to Uehara, whose face is described in the following manner in a previous chapter after he has made love to Kazuko:

When the room became faintly light, I stared at the face of the man sleeping beside me. It was the face of a man soon to die. It was an exhausted face. The face of a victim. A precious victim.[29]

Kazuko is pregnant when she writes the final note to Uehara. She declares her pride in being pregnant; the "old morality" must be swept away to make way for the revolution. "Such things as war, peace, unions, trade, politics exist in the world" so that women will give birth to healthy babies.[30] Finally she returns to the idea of the "victim."

In the present world, the most beautiful thing is a victim.
There was another little victim.
Mr. Uehara.
I do not feel like asking anything more of you, but on behalf of that little victim I should like to ask your indulgence on one thing.
I should like your wife to take my child in her arms — even once will do — and let me say then, "Naoji secretly had this child from a certain woman."[31]

Dazai does not say so explicitly, but the reader can hardly avoid the conclusion that Uehara is the "middle-aged artist" and "Suga" his wife.

The Setting Sun obviously involves Dazai personally in multiple ways. Indeed, a favorite approach to the novel by Japanese critics is to specify which aspect of Dazai the various characters represent.[32] Naoji, the drunkard and dope addict, is the Dazai of the Final Years period. Uehara the middle-aged novelist is, of course, the later Dazai. The two women characters represent certain attitudes and notions of the author: Kazuko, his ideals about revolution, especially the necessity for adults to make way for the youth who alone can bring the revolution into being; the mother, his ideals concerning the aristocracy.

The Setting Sun is also closely related to the postwar fate of Dazai's landowning family. In 1946, while the author was still living in Tsugaru, the American occupation began to execute one of its most drastic programs, the land reform. The big landowners lost their holdings and the tremendous postwar inflation wiped out even the trivial profits they had first realized from selling their land through the government. In writing of the postwar decline of the aristocracy, then, Dazai was indirectly dealing with a favorite subject of his early days, his family.

But the tables had turned. In Dazai's youth the peasants were the underdogs. Now the ex-landowners were. And Dazai's switch of allegiance (in a qualified sense) from the peasants to the aristocracy was, perhaps more than anything else, a reflection of his sympathy for the downtrodden. Naoji's final words in his testament are equally Dazai's: "I am, after all, an aristocrat."[38]

When he began writing *The Setting Sun* in the spring of 1947, Dazai might have felt a premonition that any woman pregnant by him would eventually face the task of raising the child on her own. Indeed, a reader of *The Setting Sun* might easily entertain the idea that Dazai's reckless promiscuity following the war reflects a belief that men are simply studs, and that women, from the moment of conception, are to assume all responsibilities, both pre- and post-natal. In *The Setting Sun* Dazai never brings Uehara, the biological father, together with Kazuko after their sole night of love; more strikingly, Dazai has Naoji, the "spiritual" father of Kazuko's child, commit suicide the morning after the night of conception. Thus is Kazuko left to fend for herself.

The manner in which Dazai depicts this aspect of Kazuko runs the risk of making her seem unreal. Her protestations about the importance of babies, her curious hopes for the future of the child she is carrying, her apparent lack of normal maternal instinct — all these considerations call into question the reality (perhaps Dazai would prefer the word "normality") of Kazuko as "lover" and mother-to-be. Indeed, Dazai's characterization of Kazuko and her hopes seems at times incredibly artificial. And yet, the drift of Dazai's own life during and after the composition of *The Setting Sun* prevents one from abruptly dismissing Kazuko. She may appear in some ways a theoretical construct merely; but she is involved in problems of a kind that presumably caused Dazai, too, a good deal of personal anguish.

Mindful of the stakes in Dazai's own life, many Japanese critics accept *The Setting Sun* as a serious statement of moral purpose. The reasons for this attitude go well beyond autobiographical arguments of the type suggested in the previous paragraph. We know that Dazai had been deeply interested in the New Testament for a number of years prior to his death and that he was especially drawn to Matthew, Chapter X, for certain notions underlying *The Setting Sun:*

Do not think that I have come to send peace upon the earth; I have come to bring a sword, not peace. For I have come to set a man at variance with his father and a daughter with her mother. . . . He who finds his life will lose it, and he who loses his life for my sake will find it.

It is easy to imagine Dazai being struck by these words. An old established rural family of the kind he was born into was usually a bulwark of traditional family values. Each member, integral to the group, found his raison d'être within the structure of the family. One recalls that Dazai was often indifferent or hostile to certain members of his family. There is the claim that he never knew the identity of his mother until he was in grade school, and that, on the occasion of his father's death, he felt elated as the funeral procession came into view. Later in life Dazai seldom had kind words for his oldest brother who, as the head of the family, disinherited him.

The final words of the quotation from Matthew ("He who finds his life will lose it, and he who loses his life for my sake will find it") could possibly have struck Dazai with yet greater force. As a man who had already attempted suicide at least three times, he could well have given an oddly literal interpretation to Christ's words.

Considerations other than the influence of the Bible suggest the author's seriousness of purpose. Incontestably, *The Setting Sun* deals with an impressive array of serious issues. There are the social problems confronting postwar Japan: the breakdown of aristocratic gentility, the effects of a redistribution of wealth, the jealous leveling instincts of the democratic mob. There are human and philosophic issues: filial piety, fraternal love and jealousy, benevolence, illness, suicide, and death. Indeed, the inventory is, if anything, too full for a relatively short novel.

In fact, a central problem faced by any reader of the novel — particularly the foreign reader of a translation — is whether or not Dazai was seriously examining *all this*. Probably most readers, even those who feel pity for Naoji, will be puzzled as to why he is dis-

turbed. A variety of anxieties could be cited, including Naoji's conviction that he can love only one woman, unfortunately for him, a
married one. But these anxieties are not directly rendered in the
novel. No reader can be certain that Naoji is disturbed to the degree
he claims to be. We have only Naoji's own testimony, including, it
must be admitted, his act of suicide.

Dazai's inability or reluctance to render his characters and scenes
creates other problems for the reader. Such segments of reality as the
dissolute underworld of Uehara and the humdrum domestic round
of Kazuko and her mother are sketched in relatively full detail.
Other segments of postwar Japanese society, the easygoing village
life represented by the county doctor or the realistic adaptable men-
tality of the businessman epitomized by Uncle Wada, are less firmly
delineated. Certainly the foreign reader who wishes to have some
grasp of the disparate social values represented by the mother, by
Uncle Wada, the doctor, and Uehara and to understand the relation
of these values to those of Kazuko had best put himself through a
stint of reading on postwar Japanese social history.

More important and more difficult, one should read more of Dazai
than one or two novels. A similar statement could be made about
almost any novelist worth reading, but in Dazai's case the statement
has a special meaning. A novel by Dazai, read in the context of his
other works, often turns out to be an entirely different experience
from that same novel read solely on its own terms. *The Setting Sun* is
a truly moving novel, read as one of the last of Dazai's significant
works. But one can easily imagine a reader alert to thematic or
character development, as these terms are usually understood, seeing in the novel little other than a collection of odd creatures and ill-
thought-out ideas.

Dazai did not write to create a world but to test the sincerity of his
own feelings. Reading Dazai means paying heed to the voice of
Dazai. Plot and character serve the author as an opportunity to speak
his mind at certain crucial moments, not in his own person, but in
the guise of whichever character happens to be on hand. On occasion the pace of Dazai's narrative slackens and his language assumes
a gentle tone.

I stood up. "I must be going now."
She also rose and walked, with no suggestion of reserve, to my side. "Why?"
she asked, looking at my face. Her voice had quite its ordinary timbre. She
held her head a little to the side, as if really in doubt, and looked me straight

in the eyes. In her eyes there was neither malice nor pretence. Normally, if my eyes had met hers, I would have averted them in confusion, but that one time I felt not the least particle of shyness. For sixty seconds or more, our faces about a foot apart, I stared into her eyes, feeling terribly happy. I finally said with a smile, "But — "
"He'll be back soon," she said, her face grave.[33]

    This scene in which Naoji and Suga share a moment of silence is effectively rendered in Keene's translation. But it is doubly poignant in Dazai precisely because he renders it in a tone his reader has learned to recognize as Dazai's intimate voice. One hears the author *whispering* this passage.
    On other occasions a knowledge of Dazai's biography opens a new dimension to a given scene in *The Setting Sun*. Surely, as Dazai composed the scene in which Kazuko, having broken the strap of her sandal, is kindly assisted by Uehara's wife, he must have been imagining his pathetic wife Michiko minding the children at home as her husband frittered away his time and his energies with the likes of Ota Shizuko and Yamazaki Tomie. Dazai is sometimes described as a lyrical novelist and his methods portrayed as those of the poet rather than the novelist. In reading his works, then, one must know the signals and references, one must make himself familiar with the voice. Most Dazai novels, including *The Setting Sun*, do not create a world understandable on its own terms. The most crucial context of *The Setting Sun* is not the disoriented society of postwar Japan; it is rather an earlier series of Dazai's works in which a reader discovers certain recurring personal problems and concerns and trains himself (just as when he reads a lyric poet extensively) to hear the voice of the author.
    Even the most avid reader of *The Setting Sun* would probably recall the plot of the novel in detail only with great difficulty. Most will remember that Naoji dies the morning after Kazuko spends her night with Uehara or that Kazuko goes to a beer hall with Uehara before she meets him at the bar where the raucous songfest is in progress. But the frequent use of the flashback, of letters and journals, along with the relative paucity of fully realized dramatic scenes make a reconstruction of the sequence of events in the novel extraordinarily demanding. Indeed, one of the most ambitious attempts at discerning a structure in *The Setting Sun* is posited in musical rather than dramatic terms.[34]
    It is revealing that Kanzai Kiyoshi, the critic who attempts this

particular analysis of *The Setting Sun*, makes explicit reference to
the impromptu character of Dazai's narrative method. But at the
same time Kanzai finds this a merely surface feature of Dazai's style;
if, according to Kanzai, one looks at *The Setting Sun* in the right
perspective, he clearly discerns Dazai's superior powers of construction. In Kanzai's view *The Setting Sun* is a composition of carefully
controlled movements; for example, the soft melodies of the opening
movement, representing the mother, yield to a "largo" that introduces the harsh notes associated with the aggressive daughter,
Kazuko. A critic like Kanzai emphasizes what might be termed the
fluidity of Dazai's symbolic manner; the presence of the snakes in
the garden (traditionally these curious snakes seem to be a kind of
Japanese "penates," whose appearance forbodes ill for the house) is
in harmony with the rhythms of the mother's illness and death; the
viper in Kazuko's breast flourishes at the expense of the mother's
health. Perhaps Kanzai's method of analysis will recommend itself to
the reader of Dazai who insists on *some* kind of formal unity to his
novels. It seems to me preferable to read *The Setting Sun* for the
chance to hear Dazai's voice and to regard the characters in the work
as the necessary instruments of this objective.

X   No Longer Human

Like *The Setting Sun, No Longer Human* first appeared in serial
form in a periodical. Dazai's last complete work, the novel was
published in three installments in 1948 in the June, July, and August
issues of *View*. By the time the complete work was in the public's
hands, Dazai was already dead.

To write *No Longer Human*, Dazai once again looked back over
his own experience. But many critics — both Japanese and Western
— have been especially anxious to keep the novel out of the realm of
autobiography. Okuno Tateo, in his short analysis of the work in
volume nine of *The Complete Works of Dazai Osamu*, has called *No
Longer Human* a *Bildungsroman*. Donald Keene, in the introduction to his translation of the novel, has written:

At the same time, detail after detail clearly is derived from the individual experience of Osamu Dazai himself. The temptation is strong to consider the
book as a barely fictionalized autobiography, but this would be a mistake, I
am sure. Dazai had the creative artistry of a great cameraman. His lens is
often trained on moments of his own past, but thanks to his brilliant skill in
composition and selection, his photographs are not what we would expect to

find cluttering an album. There is nothing of the meandering reminiscer about Dazai; with him all is sharp, brief and evocative.[35]

Perhaps the very form of *No Longer Human* makes such cautionary warnings especially necessary. The book opens with a short prologue and closes with an equally brief epilogue. In between, Dazai presents the reader with three notebooks of his protagonist, Yozo. The name is a familiar one to readers of Dazai. Oba Yozo, surviving his ordeal in *The Flower of Buffoonery*, finds himself once more Dazai's protagonist. Yozo — the disqualified human being — has himself attempted a love suicide at Kamakura. Even before the reader discovers this fact of Yozo's past, though, he has already made the usual tentative "identifications."[36] In the prologue to *No Longer Human* the narrator describes three photographs of Yozo. The earliest, a child's photograph, suggests "a monkey. A grinning monkey face." The monkey image, of course, calls up the early Dazai figures of such a work as "Monkey Island." The second photograph, showing Yozo in his high school or college days, is not readily identifiable in this manner. But the final photograph, by its very ambiguity, recalls the portrait of Aogi in "He Is Not What He Was": "The remaining photograph is the most monstrous of all. It is quite impossible in this one even to guess the age, though the hair seems to be streaked with gray."[37]

The three photographs are paralleled by the three notebooks that make up the main body of the novel. The notebooks, the work of the protagonist Yozo, are presented to the reader by the unnamed narrator, a novelist. A friend, the proprietress of a certain bar, has shown the novelist the notebooks — already in her safekeeping a number of years — with the thought that he might find in them material for his writing.

In the first notebook, reflecting the initial photograph, Yozo speaks of his childhood. The "monkey face" of the photograph must have been taken while Yozo was clowning. Like the young Dazai, Yozo too is a specialist at this. Again, like Dazai, Yozo forces the comedy. Once, traveling to Tokyo by train with his mother, he urinates in the spittoon in the train corridor. As he admits, he can thus pretend to childish innocence and earn laughs by submitting the story as a school composition.

In his attempts to explain the genesis of this strange comic habit, Dazai is especially explicit about one factor: a resistance in Yozo to the fact that many customs of society have no justification. "I dreaded mealtime more each day. I would sit there at the end of the table in the dimly lit room and, trembling all over as with cold, I would lift a few morsels of food to my mouth and push them in. 'Why must human beings eat three meals every single day?' ''[38] In short, the child Yozo cannot accept the arbitrariness of things.

Yozo eventually learns that he is not the only one who attempts to deceive others. One night he overhears a group of his father's friends criticizing the manner in which his father had introduced a speaker at a meeting shortly before; minutes later he watches as they compliment his father. Yozo understands their deception, since he too plays the same game. Yet, he cannot understand why practicing deception does not seem to disturb these people as it does him.

The second notebook, in association with the second photograph, tells of Yozo's life at high school in northern Honshu and at college in Tokyo. Yozo leaves his birthplace to board with relatives while attending higher school — a fact which ties the second notebook quite closely with Dazai's biography.

Yozo undergoes several unusual experiences during his higher school days. A lad named Takeichi, the school idiot, alone sees through Yozo's clowning, and accuses him of faking certain movements on the parallel bars at gym class to win a few laughs. A kind of friendship springs up between the two. Academically dull, Takeichi is privy to certain odd, but fundamental, truths. He alerts Yozo, for example, to the fact that Van Gogh's familiar self-portrait is actually the picture of a ghost. And, with this revelation, Yozo sets off on a course which recalls Dazai's decision to write as a "safety valve":

Now that I had been initiated by Takeichi into those root secrets of the art of painting, I began to do a few self-portraits. . . .
The pictures I drew were so heart-rending as to stupefy even myself. Here was the true self I had so desperately hidden. I had smiled cheerfully; I had made others laugh; but this was the harrowing reality. I secretly affirmed this self, was sure that there was no escape from it, but naturally I did not show my pictures to anyone except Takeichi.[39]

Again, like Dazai, Yozo leads a life of desperation and dissipation once he arrives in Tokyo. A fellow art student named Horiki Masao introduces him to the "mysteries of drink, cigarettes, prostitutes, pawnshops, and left-wing thought."[40] Dazai relates Yozo's experiences in these areas with an unsatisfying degree of generality.

Only in relating his affair with a bar hostess named Tsuneko, their double suicide attempt, and Yozo's subsequent survival and questioning by the police does Dazai provide the kind of circumstantial detail that will involve the reader.

The episode in which the police question Yozo following his companion's death recalls the book's early theme of deception. Yozo has bloodied his handkerchief picking at a pimple. Suddenly he coughs and pulls out the bloodied handkerchief, hoodwinking his questioner into concluding he is suffering from consumption. Just before his release he is again questioned, this time by a young official of "honest good looks." Coughing, Yozo automatically reaches for his handkerchief.

The blood stains caught my eye, and with ignoble opportunism, I thought that this cough might also prove useful. I added a couple of extra, exaggerated coughs for good measure and, my mouth still covered by the handkerchief, I glanced at the district attorney's face.
The next instant he asked with his quiet smile, "Was that real?"
Even now the recollection makes me feel so embarrassed I can't sit still. It was worse, I am sure, even than when in high school I was plummeted into hell by that stupid Takeichi tapping me on the back and saying, "You did it on purpose." These were the two great disasters in a lifetime of acting.[41]

The third notebook opens with Yozo a virtual prisoner in the home of one of his father's friends. This individual — an antique dealer named "Flatfish" — has agreed to serve as Yozo's guarantor with the police. Unable to endure Flatfish's clumsy attempts at "soul-searching," however, Yozo slips away to seek out his friend Horiki.

From this point the third notebook describes Yozo's successive experiences — first as a kept man with two different women, then as the husband of an unbelievably innocent girl, and finally as an inmate in an asylum and as the ward of an old woman.

His first mistress, an employee of a publishing firm, is a young widow named Shizuko. Yozo's relationship with her remains undeveloped in the narrative. About all the reader learns is that Shizuko finds Yozo a job drawing a cartoon serial for her publisher, a task at which he proves quite adept. More important is Yozo's relation with Shizuko's five-year-old daughter, Shigeko. Remaining in the apartment while Shizuko goes to work, Yozo becomes friendly with Shigeko. Soon Shigeko is calling him "Daddy." But, even before the reader begins to sense any hope for Yozo in this developing relation, Dazai gives the narrative a quick twist.

I [i.e., Yozo] casually changed the subject. "Shigeko, what would you like from God?"
"I would like my real daddy back."
I felt dizzy with the shock. An enemy. Was I Shigeko's enemy, or was she mine? Here was another frightening grown-up who would intimidate me. A stranger, an incomprehensible stranger, a stranger full of secrets. Shigeko's face suddenly began to look that way.
I had been deluding myself with the belief that at least Shigeko was safe, but she too was like the ox which suddenly lashes out with its tail to kill the horsefly on its flank. I knew that from then on I would have to be timid even before that little girl.[42]

From this moment Yozo's course again turns downhill. Returning one night from a drinking spree, he opens the door a crack to discover Shizuko and Shigeko happily chasing a rabbit about the apartment. Aware suddenly that the mother and daughter can be happy without him, Yozo slips away, never to return to Shizuko and Shigeko.

Yozo becomes next the kept man of the madame who runs the bar at Kyobashi. The madame of the Kyobashi bar turns out finally to be Yozo's "literary agent." For it is she who, in the epilogue of the novel, hands over Yozo's notebooks to the novelist who is presenting them to the public in *No Longer Human*.

After Yozo has degenerated a few more degrees (he is now drawing pornography), he meets a young girl of seventeen who works in the tobacco shop across the street from the bar. The girl, Yoshiko, urges Yozo to quit drinking and reform himself. Perhaps sensing that this is his final chance, Yozo decides to marry Yoshiko. But the very words describing this decision echo foreboding, not hope: "I made up my mind on the spot: it was a then-and-there decision, and I did not hesitate to steal the flower."[43]

Yozo's relation with Yoshiko turns out to be disastrous. One day she is seduced by a menial shopkeeper. Yozo of course does not play the role of the outraged husband. He realizes that Yoshiko's innocent and trusting nature (or the God who gave her that nature) is to blame; Yoshiko herself is blameless. Indeed, the experience itself cannot change her. When Yozo — having reached the breaking point — is taken to an asylum, she innocently packs his morphine and hypodermic needle. Ever trusting, she still believes Yozo's word that the morphine is an "energy-building" medicine.

The novel concludes with an epilogue which creates an entirely new perspective for Yozo's narrative. After giving the novelist the notebooks, the madame of the Kyobashi bar confesses to having read them for the first time only recently:

"Did you cry?"

"No. I didn't cry. . . . I just kept thinking that when human beings get that way, they're no good for anything."

"It's been ten years. I suppose he may be dead already. He must have sent the notebooks to you by way of thanks. Some parts are rather exaggerated I can tell, but you obviously suffered a hell of a lot at his hand. If everything written in these notebooks is true, I probably would have wanted to put him in an insane asylum myself if I were his friend."

"It's his father's fault," she said unemotionally. "The Yozo we knew was so easy-going and amusing, and if only he hadn't drunk — no, even though he did drink — he was a good boy, an angel."[44]

Okuno Tateo once expressed his conviction that *No Longer Human* was the greatest of Dazai's works. Even though such volumes as *Final Years, The New Hamlet, A Collection of Fairy Tales,* and *The Setting Sun* were forgotten, *No Longer Human,* Okuno claimed, would always be read by the Japanese. A number of reputable native critics agree with Okuno's assessment, often for the same reason: *No Longer Human,* though deficient in its treatment of the "facts" of society, confronts the "truth" of society.

No one could fault the perfect symmetry and stylistic brilliance of *No Longer Human.* The divisions of the novel are arranged with great care relative to one another; the style captures the moods of Yozo as they alternate from excitement to quiet, from extraversion to introspection. Remarkably explicit in its thematic emphasis, *No Longer Human* possibly offers more fertile ideas for the understanding of Dazai's psychic development than any of his other works.

A Western student of Dazai may well question whether the aforementioned critics are responding to *No Longer Human* as a novel or as the most incisive analysis of the problems confronting Dazai throughout his life. Such critics obviously bring a wealth of information and association on Dazai to their reading of the novel; most Western readers, on the other hand, will of necessity be acqainted only with the few English translations of Dazai's works. Most who read Donald Keene's translation of *No Longer Human* will be compelled to regard the novel as a self-contained work of art, and it is questionable whether *No Longer Human* can withstand such scrutiny any better than *The Setting Sun.*

Dazai, as the next chapter will argue, is ultimately a writer of pathos. Normally, his readers sense the pathos as an aftertaste of the author's comedy. In *No Longer Human*, Dazai appears far more anxious than usual to render pathos directly — or rather, he seems determined to let the pathos of his alter ego Yozo bare itself without the hindering presence of the author's comic spirit. In an earlier work Dazai would have created an uproarious incident of Yozo's use of the spittoon on the train to Tokyo. In *No Longer Human* Yozo consciously describes the event, including the reaction of his teacher, as a shabby episode.

The term "comedy" makes its appearance in *No Longer Human* solely as an explanation for Yozo's behavior. The sudden comic twists and exaggerated language so common to Dazai's earlier works are not conspicuous in *No Longer Human*. As early as *The Flower of Buffoonery*, Dazai had given a hint that he was disillusioned with comedy as a way of life. Perhaps *No Longer Human* deals with the "truth" (as distinct from the "facts") in showing the actual pathetic figure Dazai knew himself to be behind the mask of a clown.

XI *"Good-bye"*

"Good-bye," the title for his final work, appears at first glance a personal announcement of Dazai's imminent suicide. However, the work itself seems to militate against such an interpretation. As Keene has pointed out, Dazai seemed to be breaking new ground in writing a comic novel; he certainly does not appear to have reached the end of the line as a novelist. Again, the word "good-bye" is used so humorously in the story itself that one hesitates to give it any tragic interpretation.

And, indeed, the whole tenor of the story is whimsical. Magazine editor Tajima Shuji tries to rid himself of his mistresses with the help of an attractive woman friend. He can discourage the mistresses by introducing the attractive friend to them as his wife. But he can preserve the illusion of the attractive woman's charm only by keeping her silent, for she possesses a raucous voice. Furthermore, he is beholden to the woman for her help and must generously treat her to dinner to satisfy her enormous appetite.

Excluding the title, the twenty-odd pages of "Good-bye" contain only one hint of the author's imminent suicide. One of Tajima's literary friends, worried by the editor's overseriousness, warns: "To die from infatuation with a woman isn't a tragedy. It's a comedy. No, it's actually a farce: the height of the comical."[45]

XII *Dazai's Final Development*

Dazai's return to autobiographical modes of writing in the postwar years reflects to some extent the fact that he was once again leading a frenzied existence. Perhaps he deliberately chose such a life — as a protest against the times or as a way of reviving the urge to turn his life into literature. More likely he simply found himself cut off from his family in Kanagi and adrift in Tokyo, just as during his university days and the period preceding his engagement to Michiko. Regardless of the reasons for his dissipation, the fact that he chose to make use of his postwar life in his writing supports the contention that Dazai found in the unsavory aspects of his character his best subject for autobiographical writing.

The final autobiographical works show, in some ways, a complexity well beyond that of the earlier works. Even with such a relatively subtle work as *The Flower of Buffoonery* the reader contends with just one Dazai Osamu (in a thinly fictional guise). And, reading a series of autobiographical works from the early periods, he sees through just a single character in each work the developing image of Dazai.

The postwar works add significant complications to the role of this autobiographical figure. There are more kinds of first-person narrators, both men and women of various ages. In addition, particularly in *The Setting Sun,* Dazai appears to be "dividing" himself among a number of characters, allowing each of them to represent limited aspects of himself. The drama worked out in the novel might then be taken as representative of conflicts within Dazai's own self.

Many of the similarities and differences between the Dazai of the postwar years and the Dazai of *A Retelling of the Tales from the Provinces* and *A Collection of Fairy Tales* will be apparent to the reader. One of the most intriguing similarities is the author's refusal to permit his own ego to dominate the bulk of his works in these two periods. In retelling both the animal and human tales from earlier Japanese sources, Dazai must have examined the action through the eyes of the participating characters in order to determine his own attitude toward the characters and the manner in which he would unveil this attitude in the details of his retelling.

A reader of the postwar novels and stories suspects a similar method. Dazai confronted the need to work out more of the plot in his postwar works than in *A Retelling of the Tales from the Provinces* or *A Collection of Fairy Tales;* yet he seems to have examined with care the diverse ways in which different characters would view and react to a given set of facts and circumstances. The results of this process are quite striking. While the typical prewar "fiction" usually portrays a single character as he sees himself, the postwar fiction transcends this fixed viewpoint to describe several individuals of a social group diversely viewing one another. A reader of the postwar stories learns, for example, the viewpoint both of a husband like Dazai and of a woman married to the likes of him; the reader of *No Longer Human* must come to terms with two conceptions of Yozo, the negative figure of the notebooks and the "angel" envisioned by the madame of the Kyobashi bar.

CHAPTER 6

Conclusion

I *The Basis of Dazai's Appeal*

DAZAI Osamu first achieved wide recognition in Japan in the latter half of the 1930's. During the years of World War II, he maintained and extended his reputation. But in spite of the fact that Dazai's career had already sustain itself for a decade before 1945, Japanese readers — and to a lesser extent critics also — tend to identify the author with his life and works of the three postwar years before his death. This is an understandable tendency. Critics who regard *No Longer Human* and *The Setting Sun* as Dazai's best novels naturally emphasize the last years of Dazai's career. Readers familiar with Dazai's degenerate life following the war find in him a perfect expression of the bewilderment and nihilism often said to characterize the times.

Dazai's reputation since the time of his death has dimmed to some extent. With his life a part of history, he is safe from the sort of attack Kawabata Yasunari once made in arguing against a literary prize for Dazai on the basis of the author's immorality. At the same time, Dazai's works do not have the emotional hold on certain kinds of people they once had, and some critics such as Eto Jun have come forward to declare him a second-rate writer.

Regardless of his fortunes on the critical market, Dazai continues to be read with enthusiasm. The Chikuma Publishing Company issued approximately seven years ago a new edition of the author's complete works. Chikuma had good reason to bring out this edition, for Dazai has proved to be the company's second most popular postwar novelist. Dazai seems to be especially popular among high school and university students, perhaps the most avid readers of serious literature in Japan. The readership surveys conducted by Chikuma indicate that Dazai is bought and read by young readers in a proportion far greater than is usual for Japanese novelists.[1] A final indication of Dazai's hold on the young is reflected in the composition of the audience drawn to the memorial service held each year on the anniversary of his death on the grounds of the temple where he is buried. While the celebrities on the temple stage — many of them Dazai's friends — grow older with the passing years, the audience milling on the grounds remains perpetually young.

II *Dazai in English Translation*

The effort to introduce Dazai to the English reading public began about five years after the author's death. Between 1953 and 1960 some of Dazai's best works were receiving the attention of two of the best modern translators, Donald Keene and Edward Seidensticker. In particular, Keene's translations of "Villon's Wife," *No Longer Human*, and *The Setting Sun* have made a substantial portion of Dazai accessible to English readers.[2] In the years since 1960 English translations of a number of Dazai's stories have appeared in such journals as *Monumenta Nipponica* and *Japan Quarterly*. Presently there are no indications of a second effort to translate the remainder of Dazai into English; possibly such an effort will never be undertaken.

During the period when Dazai's most important works were being issued in English translation, several review articles portraying him as an "international writer" appeared. The most persuasive of these was an article by Earl Miner which appeared in *The Saturday Review* on the occasion of the publication of *The Setting Sun*.[3] In an effort to discern parallels between Dazai and works in Western fiction, Miner chose *Lady Chatterley's Lover* as a novel comparable in part to *The Setting Sun*. Quite dissimilar at first glance, *The Setting Sun* and *Lady Chatterley's Lover* do present certain intriguing similarities. In *The Setting Sun* Kazuko rejects her aristocratic status and appeals to a man of a lower social class to make her pregnant. Kazuko's inclination for the novelist Uehara is somewhat "theoretical" by contrast to Lady Chatterley's feeling for Mellors, but other aspects of the situation such as Mellors's lower social status are similar. Again, both Kazuko and Lady Chatterley wish to make a clean break with the sterile past and begin life in different circumstances.

Certain Japanese authors and critics have also presented Dazai as a writer capable of appealing to a foreign audience. Mishima Yukio and Yasuoka Shotaro are both reported to have testified to Dazai's high standing among the readers of his novels they encountered on journeys to the United States.[4] Yasuoka found that people in the southern states were especially impressed with *The Setting Sun.* Indeed, *The Setting Sun,* as one commentator has pointed out, can be read as the Japanese novel version of *A Streetcar Named Desire.* Southern readers can readily take Kazuko's rejection of the aristocracy as parallel to Blanche's fall in *Streetcar.* Finally, the very term "the setting sun" — a reference to the postwar decline of the Japanese aristocracy — might be applied with certain qualifications to the South that is Williams's concern in the play.

Clearly, other works in Western literature could be invoked as comparable in some degree to Dazai's works in plot, theme, and character. The works of Dazai, though, should not usually be separated from their author, and comparative approaches are valid only to the extent that they involve Dazai as author-narrator in the work under discussion.

III *Dazai, a Writer Invoking His Past*

As the preceding chapters have shown, Dazai was the type of writer who depended on the works of other writers or his own experience as the base upon which to compose his novels and stories. In relying in much of his writing on external sources more than on his imagination, Dazai was following one of the strongest trends in modern Japanese writing, the composition of autobiographical novels and stories. The tradition of the "I-novel" is usually said to have originated in 1907 with the publication of *The Quilt* by Tayama Katai, a bathetic account of a writer's involvement with a young woman anxious to study under him. Since the appearance of *The Quilt,* novelists have engaged in autobiographical writing in such numbers that some commentators have called the "I-novel" ("*shishosetsu*" in Japanese) the sole unique contribution of modern Japanese letters to world literature.

Despite their autobiographical inspiration, few if any of Dazai's works can be called *shishosetsu.* Certain writers of the *shishosetsu* (Shiga Naoya, perhaps the leading exponent of the genre, comes readily to mind) were less than admiring in their comments on Dazai's work.[5] Such a reaction is hardly surprising in view of the fact that even Dazai's first-person narratives are substantially different from the conventional *shishosetsu.*

Dazai is not a *shishosetsu* writer, primarily because he does not attempt a minute and sustained recollection and reconstruction of the past. Readers of this book might well recall familiar instances in Western letters of attempts at such minute, sustained recollection. In pure autobiography, Rousseau's *Confessions* stands as the outstanding example of such an effort, while in the area of mixed fiction-autobiography Tolstoy's *Childhood, Boyhood, Youth* represents a familiar example. And one of the best examples for American readers is Whittaker Chambers's hefty volume *Witness*. Chambers's prefatory remarks on the painful, wearying effort he undertook to recall his past with precision suggests the sort of process an intelligent American might undergo to write his own *shishosetsu*.[6]

It is questionable whether Dazai had the determination and perseverance to pursue his past in this fashion. Certain of his remarks on how he composed accounts of his past suggest a very different method. Rather than pursue it, Dazai would allow his past to come to him. Like any other person, Dazai retained a vivid memory of certain striking and important events in his past. And these memories — rather than his entire past — tend to serve his need for story material. For this reason, certain episodes occur again and again in different parts of Dazai's work, creating in some readers an exasperating sense of déjà vu.

Dazai's use of the past as a source of anecdote raises a host of critical problems. One of the commonest concerns on the part of Japanese critics and readers of the *shishosetsu* is the degree of objective truth in the narrative. One episode from recent Japanese literary and social history will suggest the sort of veracity readers of the *shishosetsu* expect from their authors. The episode was a divorce case in which the wife of a novelist successfully brought the suit for a divorce against her husband on the grounds of adultery. One of the important pieces of evidence in court was a description of her husband-author committing adultery in an "I-novel."

In Dazai's case, the problem of veracity is complicated in various ways. For many Japanese readers, the typical *shishosetsu* seems to pose the simple problem of whether or not the incidents and situations related in the novel occurred in fact. In Dazai's case, the same problem arises, but before the critic can address himself to that problem he must work his way through several other problems more germane to literary studies.

In his youth Dazai began writing works in the manner of the proletarian school — short novels with cumbersome plots narrated from the third-person omniscient point of view. In the succeeding periods of his career, Dazai frequently used first-person narration. But the first-person narrator in Dazai seldom becomes a wholly reliable one.[7] Often in his very speech the narrator of a Dazai story reveals that he is far from trustworthy. Again, even to such a relatively straightforward narrator as Kazuko in *The Setting Sun*, Dazai does not concede a monopoly on the narration. Dazai applies a check in the novel to the judgments and opinions of Kazuko by inserting (especially in "The Moonflower Journal") the voice of Naoji. Even with a relatively reliable narrator, then, Dazai appears unwilling to commit the whole truth to one character.

At times Dazai seems to mix up objective and personal modes of narration as a means of tantalizing his readers. The animal fabliau in traditional Japanese literature is as definite in import as it usually is in La Fontaine or in Chaucer. But the animals in Dazai's *A Collection of Fairy Tales* lose their conventional moral value rather thoroughly, for the personal voice of the author which any reader can recognize intervenes to upset normal expectations. Readers of "The Crackling Mountain," for example, must pay heed to the tone of Dazai's narration and accept the tale as an ironic retelling of the original.

A more intractable dilemma occurs in the epilogue to *No Longer Human*. For certain readers of the novel,[8] the brief remark by the madame of the Kyobashi bar — "The Yozo we knew was so easygoing and amusing, and if only he hadn't drunk — no, even though he did drink — he was a good boy, an angel"[9] — opens up an entirely new and ultimately believable aspect of Yozo. Yozo's estimate of himself as no longer human is false — or true, but in a sense quite different from that which he has in mind. That the novel unfolds in such a way as to allow a passing remark in the final sentence to completely alter the reader's conception of the meaning of events is a proposition very open to question. For many readers the madame's estimate of Yozo is more likely to confuse the issue.

Certain critics, exasperated by Dazai's coyness, express grave doubts about the author's veracity. Sugimori Hisahide, the author of an excellent lengthy article on Dazai's career,[10] has found some of Dazai's autobiographical claims utterly beyond belief. Sugimori finds especially preposterous Dazai's claim that he had no sexual relations with Hatsuyo until she came to live with him in Tokyo. Sugimori also expresses skepticism about the degree of illegal activity Dazai claims to have been engaged in.

This disbelief and skepticism vis-à-vis certain of Dazai's "autobiographical" statements is not based on researches that disprove or even cast doubt on Dazai's claims. Rather, Sugimori simply appears to suspect the claims Dazai makes for himself. Indeed, Sugimori has good reason for his reaction, for Dazai often writes in a fashion that invites skepticism. The famous scene from "Remembrances" quoted in an earlier chapter is a good example of writing that purports to be autobiographical but contains within itself ample justification for skepticism on a reader's part. Dazai's *bonne* Take, it will be recalled, has taken her charge to a Buddhist temple to view a painting of hell. After bringing the boy almost to tears by pointing out the punishment meted out to liars, Take takes Dazai behind the temple to continue the indoctrination.

In the graveyard on a knoll behind the temple, a large cluster of wooden *sotoba* stood alongside a hedge. In the midst of the *sotoba* there stood a black steel wheel — about the size I then imagined the full moon to be. According to Take a person turned the wheel once and let go. If the wheel did not turn back, that person would go to heaven; if it returned to its original position, the person was destined for hell.

Take would give the wheel a push, making it turn with an even sound. Invariably it stopped without turning back. But when I turned it the wheel usually returned to its starting position. I recall going alone one autumn morning to the temple. On that occasion, no matter how often I moved the wheel, fate invariably made it turn back with a clanking sound. Tired and annoyed I stubbornly pushed the wheel again and again. As evening fell I gave way to despair and left the graveyard.

Some of Dazai's best critics, Okuno Tateo in particular, place great emphasis on Dazai's abortive attempts to further the cause of communism in Japan. The sense of guilt arising from his failure drove Dazai to write and accounts, in part, for many of the odd qualities in his writing. But, as one can perhaps detect even in the above translation, Dazai seemed to enjoy casting himself as a failure — evidently to please his readers. For this reason, Yanagida Kunio, the founder of Japanese folklore studies, saw in Dazai a type very common among native farmers — the clown who deliberately makes a fool of himself in order to amuse others. The spectacle of the author mocking himself in writing parallels the boy Shuji's clowning in life. One can find episodes strewn throughout the autobiographical record: the dance Shuji would perform for his family with a huge red sweater pulled over his head or the story he wrote for a school assignment in which he claimed to have used the spittoon in the aisle of a train to urinate in. It is difficult to conceive of a reader making his way through these autobiographical reminiscences without ever questioning the author's veracity.

It is imperative to stress, at the same time, that Dazai's

characteristic autobiographical style (a style not at all confined to the works of pure autobiography) often gives the reader a feeling that the author is speaking intimately to him alone. Dazai emerges in a confiding mood, and skepticism on the reader's part seems wholly inappropriate. Dazai's rhetoric is extraordinarily effective in this area — indeed so effective that Okuno Tateo finds in this effect of intimacy the key to Dazai's popularity with younger readers.[11] Unfortunately, this effect almost defies translation. The voice of Dazai, unique and moving in Japanese, sounds somewhat prosaic and dull transcribed into English. The reader seeking an example of a comparable tone might read the opening pages of Gide's *L'Immoraliste* where Michel sets the stage for his fascinating tale beneath the stars of north Africa.

Generally speaking, Dazai's art serves the purpose of communication rather than of truth. One cannot necessarily accept Dazai's word that the facts are really what he says they are; but Dazai's performance in writing has its own value apart from the question of its truth or falsity. The image of Shuji leaving the temple grounds at dusk is both pathetic and comic because it is so exaggerated. Dazai is probably not relating an experience more or less as it occurred, but using an anecdote from childhood to suggest to the reader the sense of self-pity and self-mockery he doubtless felt within himself.

IV   *The Ambivalence of Dazai*

During the spring of 1968 a play portraying the life of Dazai Osamu was performed at the Kinokuniya Hall in the Shinjuku area of Tokyo. *An Account of Cherries*, the work of a playwright named Ima Harube, showed Dazai as both a brooding and a whimsical man. At certain moments during the performance a microphone hidden backstage was used with great effectiveness. As the actor portraying Dazai on the stage contorted his face in "spiritual anguish," the voice over the microphone, conveying the reactions of his "inner self," would announce: "*Oi! Kiza da yo! Kiza da!*" (loosely, "Knock it off, you prig!"). Certainly this presentation came very close to the center of Dazai.

From early in his youth Dazai seems to have sensed that there was something strange and abnormal about himself. Readers of this book will recall a number of incidents suggestive of abnormal behavior: the lips carved in the desk and kissed, the glancing looks at shop windows which reflected the geisha-steps Dazai was affecting, the long-distance running undertaken to clear up a dirty complexion. Readers will, in addition, recall that Dazai eventually developed through these experiences a painful awareness of himself. As he stood on a bridge one spring morning during his third year in middle school, he felt for the first time in his life that someone watching him from behind was preventing him from acting spontaneously.

Some readers may object that Dazai was overdramatizing, that a paralyzing self-consciousness could hardly spring into being so suddenly and completely. But one feels he is justified even in overstating the case, so hypnotic at times was the power over him of what some Japanese critics have called Dazai's "narcissism." One can also see here the first of the two aspects of Dazai portrayed on the stage in Ima Harube's play. The youthful Dazai in real life responded to his agonizing predicament by declaring solemnly in the next moment: "At length I let out a sigh and wondered whether I would become great." The Dazai of Ima's play would scarcely utter such words. Doubtless he would regard them as a pompous affectation likely to increase the agony of feeling self-important.

V *Literary Effects of Dazai's Ambivalence*

The strange moods and quirks of behavior on Dazai's part are, I suspect, discernible in various ways in his creative work. The task of tracing these effects in detail would require a subtle literary mind disciplined in psychological criticism and sensitive to all the nuances of Japanese style. Let it suffice for the moment to say that Dazai seems frequently uncertain of the validity and worth of his own feelings and ready to permit his works to become infected with his uncertainties.

For me two indications of Dazai's uncertainty are the occasional collapse of his style and the recurrence of puzzling details. Admittedly, the foreign observer must be cautious in expressing judgments of this kind about the works of a Japanese author. Yet such stories as "Das Gemeine," "Monkey-Face Lad," and "Retrogression" seem merely to reflect vagaries of the author's imagination, while a work like "Human Lost" seems to have been composed grudgingly. As for puzzling details, readers of the English translations of *The Setting Sun* and *No Longer Human* will possibly confess to bewildered amusement when the mother coyly urinates behind a backyard bush and when Yozo likens the front door of a home to the gate of Dante's Inferno.

It is, of course, possible to meet this problem in the manner of the following words written several years ago by an admiring student of Dazai:

Readers familiar with only a few of Dazai's works will be prone to stumble over the incongruous details. But the more thorough student of Dazai anticipates and takes delight in the quirks and oddities of his author. They assure one that Dazai, a grin on his face, is lurking behind the scene ready to take a direct hand in the goings-on of his characters. Of course some readers will find such overt intrusions unpalatable, but the reader of Dazai cannot simply overlook them. They are part of the author's signature, and one comes to expect them just as surely as he anticipates oddities in *Tristram Shandy*.[12]

One can, then, provide a rationale of sorts for the occasional haphazard quality of Dazai's writing. Yet certain passages remain embarrassingly crude, at least in contrast to the far more numerous occasions where Dazai successfully integrates his unique sense of humor with plot and style. The best contrast to the exaggerated attempts at humor is a two-word phrase, a phrase not coined by Dazai but used by him so repeatedly as a motto that one comes to regard it as his own. The expression is *umarete sumimasen* ("pardon my having been born"). Better than any other phrase, these words evoke the sense of simultaneous pity and mockery Dazai often felt toward himself.[13]

Dazai's adeptly humorous handling of certain pathetic situations can sustain itself through a series of stories. An excellent example of the author's capabilities in this respect is the series of stories involving monkeys as important characters — "Bottomless Abyss," "Monkey Island," and "The Monkey's Grave." In "Bottomless Abyss" monkeys make a brief appearance in the scene where the protagonist Kanji intercedes on behalf of a monkey ignored by the woman acrobat. In the next story, "Monkey Island" the identification is more strongly suggested. The author-protagonist, stranded on an island of monkeys, never explicitly describes himself as a monkey. But he is befriended rather naturally by one of the island monkeys. And, finally, a newspaper clipping appended to the end of the tale implies that the two companions are monkeys who escaped their cage at the London Zoo.

When the reader comes to "The Monkey's Grave," then, he is disposed to see something of Dazai in the very human monkey Kichibei. Kichibei, the pet of a young husband and wife, seems such a trustworthy creature that the young couple put him in charge of their baby Kikunosuke while they go off to visit a neighbor:

> In a little while Kichibei decided it was time for the infant's bath. So he lit a fire under the stove to boil some water — precisely, he recalled, as [the child's mother] Oran always did.
>
> When the bubbles started to rise Kichibei poured the steaming water into a basin to the very rim. Without bothering to test the water he stripped the child naked, lifted him, and — peering at his face in imitation of Oran — gently dipped the child two or three times in the basin.
>
> "Waa!" The parents, hearing the shrill cry of the scalded baby, glanced at each other and came running back to the house. The stunned Kichibei stood transfixed as the baby floated about the basin. Oran, lifting the corpse, could scarcely bear the sight of her "broiled lobster."[14]

Kichibei embodies an ideal Dazai liked to refer to as "*sabisu,*" in plain English, service. Over the years this ideal underwent strange permutations. At one point, the gifted novelist Dazai Osamu argued that writers ought deliberately to compose inferior works; a novel or story of high quality, Dazai contended (perhaps with tongue in cheek), provokes in the reader a depressing realization of how inferior are his own literary talents. But Dazai also realized that ideals would falter long before they reached such a point of absurdity. Like Kichibei in his animal innocence, the idealist often blunders in his task, thus creating a state of affairs directly counter to his hopes. Admittedly, "The Monkey's Grave" is a fable; but it is also one of Dazai's characteristic ways of saying something about himself. Indeed, in some ways, the biographical interest here is deeper than in the fictions Dazai clearly worked out from his life experience.

Dazai's use of comedy is customarily linked to his ideal of service. At times, Japanese discuss this quality of service as something highly mystical.[15] For purposes of analysis, however, it would seem advantageous to speak of two kinds of service in Dazai. One I would call "deliberate service," the other "desperate service." Even as he confronts this distinction between deliberate and desperate service, the reader of this book should keep in mind that it is sometimes difficult to determine which type of service a given piece of writing represents. If Dazai was serious in claiming that writers ought deliberately to compose inferior works, then certain of the writings which appear to be acts of desperation might have been deliberately put together in a sloppy manner.

As I indicated earlier, Dazai seems to have enjoyed playing the clown even during his youth. Most of the accounts of Dazai's childhood and youth that I have consulted describe his antics as a natural expression of youthful spirits. Occasionally, however, one encounters the suggestion that, even as a youth, Dazai intended his clowning as an act of service. Sugimori, for example, suggests that Dazai naturally came to feel he owed people (and eventually his readers) a kind of service as the son in a family paternalistic toward its tenants and the neighboring poor. The suggestion is an intriguing one, and there are at least snippets of evidence supporting it. When Dazai attended the Aomori Middle School, he received from his family a monthly allowance of one hundred yen. (A beginning teacher at the school received a monthly salary of thirty to forty yen.) Dazai continued to live off an allowance from his family during his higher school and university days and even beyond graduation. Some commentators suggest that Dazai used a substantial portion of his allowance to help his poorer classmates as a means of allaying his own guilt feelings over this undeserved beneficence; a critic like Sugimori, on the contrary, appears to see Dazai's generosity toward his friends as a form of patronage. Just as the wealthy landlord had to look after the welfare of his tenants, the landlord's son was obligated to alleviate the hardships of those poorer than himself. Sugimori regards Dazai's youthful clowning as a parallel service.[16] It should be noted that Sugimori's notion of the initial inspiration for Dazai's clowning corresponds somewhat with that of Yanagida Kunio, at least to the extent of locating that inspiration in the customs and practices of Dazai's birthplace.

Even after Dazai left Kanagi he continued his career as clown — in his writing if not in his behavior. And during his extended residence in Tokyo, it appears that he became more and more familiar with an art that helped him maintain and develop his comic gift. This art — almost unknown to the West — is a traditional type of storytelling and pantomime known as *rakugo*.

Rakugo storytellers practice their act seated on a cushion before an audience in the "Yose" theater. The storyteller will simultaneously mimic and narrate a comic situation — for example, two old women in a public bathhouse, each of whom insists that the other use the single bar of soap first. Gesturing with his fan and arms and adopting the speech and accent appropriate to his characters, the storyteller develops the situation into a skit. The comedy depends so heavily on punning and rapid-fire speech that a foreign observer, of course, lacking long experience in listening to the stories, finds it almost impossible to follow.

Dazai was deeply interested in *rakugo*. To my knowledge, he did not attend the "Yose" theater, at least with any regularity. But the depth of his interest in this art reveals itself in a passage from Dan Kazuo's *The Story of Dazai Osamu*. According to Dan, Dazai kept only a small supply of books at home. He read only occasional volumes even of those authors he admired — Ueda Akinari, Saikaku, and Basho especially among Japanese writers. But Dazai collected *rakugo* texts more thoroughly, including the complete works of the nineteenth-century master Encho, and he read through them with regularity and enthusiasm.[17]

The diverse remarks of Yanagida, Sugimori, and Dan concerning the possible inspiration and techniques of Dazai's comic art imply a conception of "deliberate" service. Dazai, according to this conception, is a writer (or narrator) of comic skits who employs his talents to entertain an audience of Japanese during several rather somber decades of their history. By and large, I have read Dazai's works in this spirit, and have described him in the foregoing pages principally as this kind of writer.

There are several reasons for suggesting that this is an incomplete view. In a number of works Dazai does not appear to have the comedy under control, as a *rakugo* storyteller should. He often seems perversely eccentric and, on a few occasions, absolutely inane. Each time he changes the narrative point of view in a radical and bewildering way or simply utters in his own person that the story is breaking down, Dazai seems to be admitting that his own self-consciousness or impatience is more important than his art.

Still, these occasional failures do not bulk too large in the whole corpus of Dazai's works, and they compromise only in a slight way the judgment that Dazai is a superb comic writer. More important for the foreign reader's final consideration of the nature of Dazai's writing is the reaction one hears from many mature Japanese readers: that Dazai's writing, while outwardly comic, has a kind of deep, intangible sadness within.

Certain passages dealt with in earlier chapters, most notably the passage referring to writing as a "safety valve," suggest that Dazai undertook his writing career out of desperation. There is evidence showing that Dazai often considered himself a misfit and a failure; there is evidence that he sensed that others must feel the same way about themselves; and, finally, there is evidence that he wrote in order to establish a bond among these outcasts. In addition to the explicit evidence, there is the intimate tone of much of the writing, a tone that creates in the reader a sense that Dazai is speaking specially and only to him.

Such evidence suggests that Dazai wrote not only to serve his readers but also to console himself. That others would read him (and by reading him, *hear* him) meant that there were after all *others like him*. Dazai's fears about whether he would be accepted as a writer — whether he would, for example, win the Akutagawa Prize — do not, I believe, reflect a desire for public recognition and success. They reflect instead Dazai's concern as to whether there were others like him. His immense popularity in the aftermath of the war suggests that many Japanese readers found in Dazai the sort of consolation and sense of identity that the author himself was groping for. That his continuing popularity has depended to a great extent on youthful readers is precisely what one would expect. Many high school and university students will find in Dazai a reflection of their own identity fears and derive a certain gratification from discovering that someone else has these same fears.

Some Japanese critics see in Dazai's appeal to the young an indication of his limitation as a writer. At times, these critics suggest that Dazai himself felt this limitation so strongly that he despaired of ever developing a more mature vision. It was this despair which eventually led to his suicide.

VI *Dazai's Suicide*

Despite the arguments to the contrary, I see Dazai as a writer who insisted on some margin for the comic, especially the incongruously comic, in the midst of the pathetic and tragic. The best characterization of Dazai as a man remains the self-pitying, self-mocking expression *"umarete sumimasen"* ("pardon my having been born"). In thinking about the various possible reasons for Dazai's suicide, I find myself searching for motives appropriate to my own view of what sort of man Dazai was.

Most critics and scholars of Dazai eventually find themselves wondering aloud about the motives for his suicide. One indispensable reference in this search is a moving essay by Dazai's friend, the literary and social critic, Kamei Katsuichiro. Kamei wrote the essay (briefly treated in the previous chapter) in a mood of reminiscing sometime in the interval of four or five days from the time Dazai disappeared to the moment his body was recovered from the canal:

> For me Dazai was a cheerful friend, full of humor. Sometimes, just to entertain us, he would dream up some absurd scheme. Once he said he would disappear for a few days, as though he intended to commit suicide. Then his teachers, friends, and critics would begin writing their memories and criticizing him. Probably some who had acted like friends would turn out to be enemies. Probably others would quickly prove their friendship.
> Then he would nonchalantly return and read his obituaries, without skipping one.[18]

Dazai, in fact, liked on occasion to disappear for two or three days. Readers of Dan Kazuo's *The Story of Dazai Osamu* will readily sympathize with the author of that work, for he was invariably called upon to search out the whereabouts of his wayward friend. Dazai, as his remarks to Kamei reveal, was acutely aware that his friends would worry about his disappearance. Perhaps Dazai disappeared at times deliberately to provoke their concern, almost in fact to tease them. Perhaps, after returning to society so regularly after earlier suicide attempts, he welcomed death as a way of breaking the monotony of return. Dazai could well have conceived such a thought. And the student of Dazai in his turn can conceive all sorts of comic implications in the manner and circumstances of his author's death. A man who found comedy so readily within the context of tragedy as Dazai did, would not, I think, regard such efforts as a slur on his good name.

Notes and References

I have used as my basic text for this study the Chikuma edition of 1962 - 1963, *Dazai Osamu Zenshu (The Complete Works of Dazai Osamu)*. This collection, edited by Okuno Tateo, was published in twelve volumes. A final volume of essays, also edited by Okuno, appeared as part of the collection in 1963. I will use the abbreviation *Works* in the following notes for this collection.

I have given Japanese names with the surname first.

Chapter One

1. See discussion below, pp. 152 - 53.
2. G. T. Shea, *Left-Wing Literature in Japan*, p. 79.
3. Okuno Tateo, *Dazai Osamu Ron*, p. 42.
4. *Works*, I, p. 17.
5. *Ibid.*, pp. 18 - 19.
6. *Ibid.*, p. 37.
7. *Ibid.*
8. "Bottomless Abyss" represents a literal translation of the characters of the title. It should be borne in mind that the word also refers to that part of a kabuki theater beneath the revolving stage.
9. *Works*, XII, pp. 163 - 64.
10. *Ibid.*, pp. 125 - 26.
11. *Ibid.*, p. 154.
12. *Ibid.*, p. 160.
13. *Ibid.*
14. On reliable narrators, see chapter eight in Wayne Booth, *The Rhetoric of Fiction*.
15. *Works*, XII, p. 224.
16. *Ibid.*, p. 266.

Chapter Two

1. *Works*, IV, p. 45.
2. *Ibid.*, pp. 46 - 47.
3. *Ibid.*, VIII, pp. 164 - 65.

4. *Ibid.*, IV, p. 50.
5. *Ibid.*, I, p. 10.
6. *Ibid.*, pp. 10 - 11.
7. *Ibid.*, p. 12.
8. *Ibid.*, p. 11.
9. *Ibid.*, p. 8.
10. *Ibid.*, p. 11.
11. *Ibid.*, p. 18.
12. *Ibid.*, p. 22.
13. *Ibid.*, p. 46.
14. *Ibid.*, p. 36.
15. *Ibid.*, p. 37.
16. Donald Keene, "The Artistry of Dazai Osamu," *The East-West Review*, Winter, 1965, p. 236.
17. *Ibid.*
18. *Works*, I, p. 144.
19. *Ibid.*, p. 150.
20. *Ibid.*, p. 159.
21. *Ibid.*, p. 162.
22. *Ibid.*, p. 239.
23. The reader interested in the Japanese tradition of *joshi*, or double suicide committed by a pair of lovers, should consult Donald Keene's study and translation, *Major Plays of Chikamatsu* (New York: 1961).
24. *Works*, I, p. 234.
25. *Ibid.*, p. 198.
26. *Ibid.*, pp. 212 - 13.
27. *Ibid.*, p. 237.
28. Keene, "Dazai Osamu," pp. 241 - 42.

Chapter Three

1. See Fukuda Kiyota and Itagaki Shin, *Dazai Osamu*, p. 60.
2. Indeed, Ibuse, a writer of considerable stature, is reputed to have corrected the provincialisms in Dazai's early work.
3. See p. 39.
4. The Akutagawa Literary Prize is awarded each year for the most outstanding piece of fiction or drama by an unknown writer. The prize commemorates the great short story writer Akutagawa Ryunosuke (1892 - 1927).
5. *Works*, II, p. 49.
6. Okuno Tateo, *Dazai Osamu Ron*, p. 67.
7. *Works*, II, p. 74.
8. *Ibid.*, p. 83. The writers Dazai mentions are Satomi Ton and Shimazaki Toson, both well-known novelists.
9. Fukuda and Itagaki, p. 68.
10. The Japanese title, "*Obasute*," refers to a widespread Japanese legend. The legend varies considerably in its details, but invariably shows an old person being left on a mountainside to die.

11. In the event of an arranged marriage, the parents and the go-between who brought the parties together would be held responsible for the fate of the marriage. For a detailed description of some of the considerations involved in arranging such a marriage, see Richard K. Beardsley, John W. Hall, and Robert E. Ward, *Village Japan* (Chicago: 1959), pp. 316 - 18.

12. Fukuda and Itagaki, p. 73.

13. *Ibid.*, p. 74.

14. *Works*, III, p. 316.

15. Fukuda and Itagaki, p. 82.

16. *Works*, III, p. 311.

17. Mori Ogai (1862 - 1922) managed a considerable output of novels, stories, essays, and translations while pursuing the busy life of surgeon general in the Japanese army.

18. *Works*, III, p. 312.

19. *Ibid.*, II, p. 26.

20. *Ibid.*, pp. 14 - 15.

21. *Ibid.*, p. 20.

22. *Ibid.*, p. 21.

23. *Ibid.*, pp. 127 - 28.

24. *Ibid.*, III, p. 185.

25. Joseph Anderson and Donald Richie, *The Japanese Film: Art and Industry* (Tokyo: 1959), p. 320.

26. *Works*, IV, pp. 234 - 35.

27. Both this and the previous quotation are from *Works*, IV, p. 210.

28. "Self-pity is not and has not been considered as reprehensible an emotion in Japan as it is considered in the West." Edward Seidensticker, introduction to *The Gossamer Years* (Tokyo: 1964), p. 29.

Chapter Four

1. Donald Keene, "The Artistry of Dazai Osamu," p. 250.

2. *Ibid.*, p. 248.

3. *Ibid.*, pp. 239 - 40.

4. See Edward Seidensticker, *Kafu the Scribbler* (Stanford: 1956), p. 170.

5. Fukuda Kiyohito and Itagaki Shin, *Dazai Osamu*, p. 92.

6. The *Fudoki* is an eighth century A.D. collection of records detailing the topography and agricultural products of various regions in Japan at that time.

7. On the use of this word see Ito Sei, *Shosetsu no Ninshiki* (Tokyo: 1958), p. 37.

8. *Works*, VI, p. 296.

9. *Hinbyo*, or "poverty illness," plays on the Japanese word for poverty, *binbo*.

10. *Works*, VI, p. 175.

11. *Ibid.*, p. 180.

12. *Nise Monogatari, A Tale of Fraud*, parodies the title *Ise Monogatari, The Tales of Ise*, a poem romance of the tenth century. In *The "Gay" Tale*

of the Heike, "the long complex epic of the fall of the Taira Clan (Heike) has dwindled to an ukiyo adventure." Howard Hibbett, *The Floating World in Japanese Fiction* (New York: 1960), p. 91.

13. See Ihara Saikaku, *Five Women Who Loved Love*, translated by William Theodore De Bary (Tokyo: 1956).

14. Ivan Morris, in his book on Saikaku, conveys a sense of the ambiguity of the author's attitude toward the samurai ethic. Apropos of Saikaku's volumes *A Record of Traditions of the Warrior's Way, Tales of the Knightly Code of Honour*, and *New Records of Strange Events*, Morris writes: "All these were collections of independent stories, dealing mainly with the traditional themes of loyalty, honour, and revenge, but presenting them in a modern, realistic way, so that we are struck not only by the noble side of the warrior's ethic, but by its futile and even pathetic aspects." See Ihara Saikaku, *The Life of an Amorous Woman*, edited and translated by Ivan Morris (Norfolk: 1963), p. 27.

15. *Works*, VI, p. 194.

16. *Ibid.*, pp. 195 - 96.

17. *Ibid.*, pp. 246 - 47.

18. *Ibid.*, p. 252.

19. *Ibid.*, VII, p. 30.

20. *Ibid.*, p. 32.

21. *Ibid.*, p. 128.

22. *Ibid.*, p. 104.

23. *Ibid.*, p. 54.

24. *Ibid.*, pp. 45 - 46.

25. See Basho, *The Narrow Road to the Deep North and Other Travel Sketches*, translated by Nobuyuki Yuasa (Suffolk: Bungay, 1966).

26. Mock Joya claims that the badger in Japanese folklore, despite its mischievous ways, is never a malicious animal, as the fox often is. See Mock Joya, *Things Japanese* (Tokyo: 1960), pp. 174 - 75.

27. A. B. Mitford, *Tales of Old Japan* (Tokyo: 1966), p. 214.

Chapter Five

1. Fukuda Kiyohito and Itagaki Shin, *Dazai Osamu*, p. 93.

2. *Ibid.*, p. 94.

3. *Ibid.*, pp. 96 - 97.

4. *Ibid.*, p. 102.

5. In his introduction to the translation of *No Longer Human* Donald Keene gives considerable emphasis to this point.

6. Kamei Katsuichiro, "Omoide," in *Dazai Osamu: Gendai no Esupuri*, edited by Saeki Shoichi, pp. 174 - 82.

7. *Works*, VIII, p. 160.

8. *Ibid.*, p. 165.

9. *Ibid.*, p. 172.

10. *Ibid.*, p. 168.

11. *Ibid.*, p. 182.

12. For Okuno Tateo's opinion see *Works*, XI, p. 394.

13. Fukuda and Itagaki claim that "Villon's Wife" is the most critically acclaimed of all Dazai's works. See Fukuda and Itagaki, p. 181. For an English translation see *Modern Japanese Literature*, edited by Donald Keene (New York: 1956), pp. 394 - 414.

14. Keene, *Modern Japanese Literature*, p. 414.

15. *Works*, IX, p. 50.

16. Keene, *Modern Japanese Literature*, p. 398.

17. *Works*, IX, p. 280.

18. *Ibid.*, p. 281.

19. See Donald Keene *Major Plays of Chikamatsu* (New York: 1961), pp. 381 - 425.

20. This summary is intended primarily to bring out those aspects of the play relevant to Dazai's story. For a more comprehensive summary see Aubrey S. and Giovanna M. Halford, *The Kabuki Handbook* (Tokyo: 1956), pp. 268 - 76.

21. On this term see Halford, p. 439.

22. *Works*, IX, p. 201.

23. Tsushima Shuji is, of course, Dazai Osamu. See first page of Preface.

24. On the land reform see Ronald Dore, *Land Reform in Japan* (London: 1959).

25. *The Setting Sun*, translated by Donald Keene, p. 54.

26. *Ibid.*, p. 179.

27. *Ibid.*, p. 181.

28. *Ibid.*, pp. 102 - 103.

29. *Ibid.*, pp. 160 - 61.

30. *Ibid.*, p. 186.

31. *Ibid.*, p. 188.

32. For Okuno Tateo's scheme, see *Works*, IX, p. 396.

33. *The Setting Sun*, p. 162.

34. Kanzai Kiyoshi, "Shayo no Mondai." This essay is most readily accessible in the *kenkyu* volume of Dazai's *Complete Works*. See pp. 109 ff. in that volume of the 1962 - 1963 Chikuma edition of *Works*.

35. Quoted from Keene's introduction to *No Longer Human* (London, 1953), p. 13. Quotations from the novel are taken from this translation of *No Longer Human*.

36. For the Oba Yozo of *The Flower of Buffoonery*, pp. 55 - 58.

37. *No Longer Human*, p. 16.

38. *Ibid.*, p. 20.

39. *Ibid.*, pp. 48 - 49.

40. *Ibid.*, p. 51.

41. *Ibid.*, p. 84.

42. *Ibid.*, p. 104.

43. *Ibid.*, p. 118.

44. *Ibid.*, pp. 153 - 54.

45. *Works*, IX, p. 373.

Chapter Six

1. This information was given to me in 1967 by a representative of the Chikuma Publishing Company. During the conversation on that occasion, the representative also mentioned that the best-selling novelist was Tanizaki Junichiro.

2. Translations of Dazai's best-known works are available in several European languages, especially French.

3. Earl Miner, "A Private Revolution," *Saturday Review*, 39:14 (September 29, 1956), pp. 14 - 15.

4. The information in this paragraph comes from a booklet published by Chikuma with volume eleven of the 1968 edition of the *Dazai Osamu Zenshu*. The booklet consists of an interview in Japanese conducted by the critic Okuno Tateo with V. H. Viglielmo and myself.

5. The feeling toward Shiga on Dazai's part seems to have been mutual. Dazai once wrote of Shiga:

What everyone says is so "fine" in his works amounts to nothing more than a man's conceit, the courage of a bully. . . . If he writes that he has broken wind it will be published in large print — and we are supposed to read this with a solemn look on our faces. What a lot of nonsense!

Quoted from William Ferguson Sibley, "The Shiga Hero," dissertation, University of Chicago, 1971, p. 12.

6. It is difficult to imagine the sort of process the Japanese writer might undergo to accomplish the same purpose. Any American who spends a substantial time in Japan living in close contact with Japanese must be struck with the ease and facility with which large numbers of the people can describe a great multitude of their past experiences. I believe that a study of the cultural reasons for this phenomenon and the techniques used to evoke the anecdotal past would contribute greatly to our understanding of modern Japanese fiction.

7. For a discussion of the reliable narrator, see Wayne Booth, *The Rhetoric of Fiction*. Part II especially addresses itself to this matter.

8. The translator of the work, Donald Keene, would appear to be one of these readers. See the "Translator's Introduction" to *No Longer Human*.

9. *No Longer Human* (London, 1953), p. 154.

10. Sugimori Hisahide, "Kuno No Kishu," *Bessatsu Bungei Shunju* (1967), pp. 140 - 92. This was published as a special New Year's edition.

11. This point came up several times in conversations I held with Okuno in the winter of 1967 - 1968, conversations which contributed greatly to my understanding of Dazai.

12. Quoted from my article "Dazai Osamu: Comic Writer," *Critique*, XIII (1970), 83.

13. It should be pointed out that Ima Harube in his play *An Account of Cherries* is dramatizing precisely this aspect of Dazai. The phrase "*umarete*

sumimasen" is translated as "forgive me that I was born" by Miyoshi Masao in *Accomplices of Silence: The Modern Japanese Novel* (Berkeley & Los Angeles: U. of California Press, 1974), p. 122.

14. *Works,* VI, pp. 195 - 96.

15. Indeed, when I presented some of the ideas in this chapter in a lecture before a Japanese audience, I was challenged by a matronly listener who claimed that a foreigner could not possibly understand the meaning of the term "service" as used by the Japanese.

16. Sugimori, p. 155.

17. For Dan's account of Dazai's interest in *rakugo,* see *Shosetsu Dazai Osamu,* p. 47.

18. See Kamei Katsuichiro, "Omoide," in *Dazai Osamu: Gendai no Espuri,* edited by Saeki Shoichi, p. 175.

Selected Bibliography

PRIMARY SOURCES

1. In Japanese
The following list of Dazai's writings has been limited to complete works
sufficiently important to be included in the chronology at the beginning of
this book:

Bannen (Final Years). Tokyo: Sunakoya Shobo, 1906.
Doke No Hana (The Flower of Buffoonery). Tokyo: Shinchosha, 1937.
Dasu Gemaine (Das Gemeine). Tokyo: Jinbun Shobo, 1940.
Fugaku Hyakkei (One Hundred Views of Mount Fuji). Tokyo: Jinbun
      Shobo, 1940.
Hashire Merosu (Run Melos). Tokyo: Kawade Shobo, 1940.
Tokyo Hakkei (Eight Views of Tokyo). Tokyo: Jitsugyo No Nihonsha, 1941.
Human Lost. Tokyo: Jitsugyo No Nihonsha, 1941.
Kojiki Gakusei (Beggar-Student). Tokyo: Jitsugyo No Nihonsha, 1941.
Kakekomi Uttae (The Indictment). Tokyo: Getsuyoso, 1941.
Tsugaru. Tokyo: Koyama Shoten, 1944.
Shinshaku Shokoku Banashi (A Retelling of the Tales from the Provinces).
      Tokyo: Seikatsusha, 1945.
Otogi Zoshi (A Collection of Fairy Tales). Tokyo: Chikuma Shobo, 1945.
Biyon No Tsuma (Villon's Wife). Tokyo: Chikuma Shobo, 1947.
Shayo (The Setting Sun). Tokyo: Shinchosha, 1947.
Ningen Shikkaku (No Longer Human). Tokyo: Chikuma Shobo, 1948.

2. In translation
The following list comprises the more substantial works of Dazai available
in translation in European languages. For further information the reader
should consult the bibliography, *Modern Japanese Literature in Western
Translations*, published by the International House of Japan Library.

a. Novels

KEENE, DONALD. *No Longer Human.* London: Peter Owen Ltd., 1953; and
      New York: New Directions, 1958.
———. *The Setting Sun.* New York: New Directions, 1956.

b. Stories

GANGLOFF, ERIC. "Leaves." *Chicago Review*, 20 (1968), 31 - 41.

HARPER, THOMAS. "Metamorphosis." *Japan Quarterly*, vol. 17, no. 3 (1970), 285 - 88.

KEENE, DONALD, "Villon's Wife." *Modern Japanese Literature*. Ed. Donald Keene. New York: Grove Press, 1956, pp. 398 - 414.

MORRIS, IVAN. "The Courtesy Call." *Modern Japanese Stories*. Ed. Ivan Morris. Tokyo: Charles E. Tuttle, 1962, pp. 465 - 80.

MOTOFUJI, FRANK. "A Sound of Hammering." *Japan Quarterly*, vol. 16, no. 2 (1969).

NATHAN, JOHN. "Romanesque." *Japan Quarterly*, vol. 12, no. 3 (1965), 331 - 46.

SEIDENSTICKER, EDWARD. "Cherries." *Encounter*, vol. 1, no. 1 (1953), 23 - 28.

———. "Osan." *Japan Quarterly*, vol. 5, no. 4, (1958), 478 - 87.

———. "Of Women." *Atlantic Monthly*, (January, 1955), pp. 145 - 47.

SWANN, THOMAS E. "Fallen Flowers." *Monumenta Nipponica*, vol. 24, no. 1 - 2 (1969), 168 - 79.

———. "A Snowy Night's Tale." *Monumenta Nipponica*, vol. 22, no. 1 - 2 (1967), 211 - 15.

SECONDARY SOURCES

The following list is extremely selective. It includes in the main the materials I made greatest use of in preparing this study.

BESSHO NAOKI. *Dazai Osamu no Kotoba*. Tokyo: Hoga Shoten, 1963. Commentary based on certain sayings of Dazai.

BOOTH, WAYNE. *The Rhetoric of Fiction*. Chicago: The University of Chicago Press, 1961. Indispensable critical work for the student of the novel.

DAN KAZUO. *Shosetsu Dazai Osamu*. Tokyo: Shinbisha, 1964. Fascinating sketch of Dazai's life by one of his closest friends.

FUKUDA KIYOHITO and ITAGAKI SHIN. *Dazai Osamu*. Tokyo: Shimizu Shoin, 1966.

KAMEI KATSUICHIRO. *Buraiha no Inori*. Tokyo: Shinbisha, 1964. As usual Kamei is primarily interested in the philosophical and social dimensions of his subject. Of the books treating Dazai in this respect, his is one of the best.

KEENE, DONALD. "The Artistry of Dazai Osamu." *The East-West Review*, Winter, 1965, pp. 241 - 53. Brief but interesting commentary covering the major phases of Dazai's career.

KOYAMA KIYOSHI, ed. *Dazai Osamu*. Tokyo: Chikuma Shobo, 1964. Essays by a variety of hands supplemented by a good collection of photographs revealing various aspects of Dazai's life.

OKUNO TATEO, ed. *Dazai Osamu Kenkyu*. Tokyo: Chikuma Shobo, 1963. A collection of essays by leading critics of Dazai.

————. *Dazai Osamu Ron.* Tokyo: Shinyusha, 1966. Probably the closest thing to a definitive study of a subject hard to define.

OTA SHIZUKO. *Shayo Nikki.* Tokyo: Hamu Shobo, 1948. The diary of one of Dazai's mistresses. Important source for the study of *The Setting Sun.*

SAEGUSA YASUTAKA. *Dazai Osamu: Narushishizumu to Ai.* Tokyo: Yushindo, 1962. An analytic study dealing with such areas as Dazai's philosophy and his use of Japanese classical literature.

————. *Dazai Osamu to sono Shogai.* Tokyo: Shinbisha, 1965. Like the previous book, very serious in tone and purpose.

SAEKI SHOICHI, ed. *Dazai Osamu.* Tokyo: Sanyosha, 1966. Especially interesting for its inclusion of Kamei's essay on Dazai's final disappearance.

SAKO JUNICHIRO. *Dazai Osamu ni okeru Decadansu no Rinri.* Tokyo: Gendai Bungeisha, 1958. A good example of a study that takes Dazai too seriously.

————. *Dazai Osamu Ron.* Tokyo: Shinbisha, 1958. Again neglects the comic in Dazai.

SEIDENSTICKER, E. G. *Gendai Nihon Sakka Ron.* Tokyo: Shinchosha, 1964. The essay on Dazai is concerned more with Dazai's faults than his virtues. However, in the postface to his book, Seidensticker refers to Dazai as a "superb comic writer."

SHEA, G. T. *Left-wing Literature in Japan.* Tokyo: Hosei University Press, 1964. A detailed historical survey. Plenty of information but very little perspective.

SUGIMORI HISAHIDE. "Kuno no Kishu." *Bessatsu Bungei Shunju,* 1967, pp. 140 - 92. This volume was published as a special New Year's edition.

YAMAGISHI GAISHI. *Ningen Dazai Osamu.* Tokyo: Chikuma Shobo, 1962. Vivid account of Dazai by another friend. Uncovers the perverse side of Dazai's character.

Index